THE TEACHER'S
4
IDEA
BOOK

# THE ESSENTIAL
# PARENT
# WORKSHOP
# RESOURCE

D1377243

## Other Titles in the Series

## Related High/Scope Press Preschool Publications

*Available from*
### High/Scope® Press
A division of the
High/Scope Educational Research Foundation
600 North River Street, Ypsilanti, MI 48198-2898
ORDERS: phone (800)40-PRESS, fax (800)442-4FAX
e-mail: *press@highscope.org*  Web site: *www.highscope.org*

THE TEACHER'S
4
IDEA
BOOK

# THE ESSENTIAL
# PARENT WORKSHOP
# RESOURCE

## Michelle Graves

HIGH/SCOPE® PRESS

Ypsilanti, Michigan

Published by

High/Scope® Press

**A division of the High/Scope Educational Research Foundation**
**600 North River Street**
**Ypsilanti, Michigan 48198-2898**
**(734)485-2000, fax (734)485-0704**
*press@highscope.org*

Holly Barton, *High/Scope Press Editor*
Margaret FitzGerald, Metaphor Marketing Inc., *Cover design, text design, and production*

**Library of Congress Cataloging-in-Publication Data**

Graves, Michelle, 1952-
    The essential parent workshop resource : the teacher's idea book 4 / Michelle Graves.
        p. cm.
    Includes index.
        1. Early childhood education--Parent participation--United States. 2. Parent and child--United States. 3. Early childhood education--Activity programs--United States.  I. Title.

    LB1139.35.P37 G72 2000
    371.19'2--dc21

                                                                    99-052715


Printed in the United States of America
10 9 8 7 6

# Contents

# Preface

The first three books in the *Teacher's Idea Book* series offered educators practical teaching ideas and strategies to use in the early childhood classroom. Although the focus of the current book is on interaction with the *parents* of young children rather than with the children themselves, it is our hope that the children ultimately will benefit from the partnership formed between families and teachers and from the application of High/Scope principles in the home and community.

The workshop plans presented in *The Essential Parent Workshop Resource* are intended to provide a strong framework for educators who work with parents of preschool-aged children. Since each group of parents has its own unique interests, concerns, and viewpoints on issues, workshop facilitators can use this book as a starting point for planning a workshop series around the particular needs of their group of parents.

Many High/Scope staff members contributed to the development of this book. Mary Hohmann and Beth Marshall were instrumental in setting the overall tone of the book and in designing the format of the workshop plans. They also provided constant feedback and support as the workshop plans and ideas unfolded. David Weikart, Ann Epstein, and Lynn Taylor provided further administrative support and helpful feedback on content. Rod Snodgrass, Eileen Storer, Suzanne Gainsley, and Rosie Lucier modeled the High/Scope active learning philosophy as they taught the children in the High/Scope Demonstration Preschool and field-tested some of these plans in actual parent meetings. The sensitivity of these teachers to children and parents and to all the needs and demands families face was a constant source of inspiration to me. Holly Barton's skillful editing of words and gentle questioning about content issues ("Did you mean . . . ?") helped clarify the ideas I wanted to communicate. I also appreciate Margaret FitzGerald's persistence in designing an engaging cover and layout for the book. Finally, I would like to acknowledge the importance of my own preschool-aged children, Christopher and Joshua, and my husband, Keith, in helping shape the ideas presented in this book.

# Introduction

*"It seems like my child has more trouble making friends than the other children in the class. Every time I come to pick her up she's always by herself, while the other children are busy working together. I suppose I could just wait until the scheduled conference time to find out if there really is a problem."*

*"I noticed some of the other parents hovering around the door at drop-off time today, and I couldn't help but overhear them talking about how hard it is to get their children to bed at a reasonable time without a lot of fussing and crying. Boy, could I relate!"*

> — Comments overheard from parents of preschoolers at the beginning of a new school year

*"I know it shouldn't, but it really irritates me when parents send children to school tired, sick, or full of a breakfast of soda pop and donuts. Don't they know how physical health impacts their child's ability to pay attention and learn new things?"*

*"On top of all the other demands, they are adding parent meeting times to our list of job requirements this year. I feel much more comfortable working with the children than I do with their parents."*

> — Comments overheard from early childhood teachers at the beginning of a new school year

## Why a Book on Parent Workshops?

Feelings such as those expressed above—reluctance to confer with a child's teacher, resentment over having to conduct parent meetings—are not uncommon among parents and early childhood educators. Although parents and teachers often desire to collaborate in the process of educating and raising young children, putting the ideal into practice can be difficult and demanding for all concerned. We have created this collection of parent workshops in the hope of making this task easier and more rewarding for everyone involved. Although we assume that the workshops will most often be presented by classroom teachers, they are also suitable for presentation by trainers, administrators, social workers, and other early childhood professionals. Following are two important ways we believe the ideas presented in this book can benefit all adults who facilitate workshops for parents of preschool-aged children.

- **Build a strong partnership between parents and school personnel.** To cooperate successfully in educating and raising children, parents and professionals have to be willing to listen to one another and to share their unique knowledge and experience with one another. Such a relationship enables each side to more readily clarify any misunderstandings and misconceptions that may occur. While exchange of information can and does occur during daily drop-off and pick-up times, it is also beneficial to have a time set aside specifically for a more thorough discussion of topics of interest to both parents and educators. In the "Reading at Home" workshop, for example, parents discuss their own reading habits and the criteria they use when choosing books for their children. They then evaluate several storybooks using additional criteria suggested by the teacher. Through these activities teachers learn what kind of print environment children are used to at home, and parents may expand their understanding of what makes a book valuable and rewarding for young children.

*Parents and teachers often talk informally at the beginning and end of the school day, but parent workshops provide opportunities to discuss important issues in depth.*

- **Enhance parents' awareness of how the High/Scope Preschool Curriculum supports children's needs and interests and how to apply High/Scope principles in everyday situations.** The High/Scope educational approach, developed and refined over the past 40 years, offers strategies and techniques for interacting with children in ways that help them become independent thinkers and accomplished problem solvers. Parents are often curious about the High/Scope approach, perhaps from observing the principles in action in the classroom or hearing some of the special terms from their child ("Hey, Dad, guess what we did for recall today!"), and we believe that it is important to share the "whats" and "whys" of the curriculum with them. The workshop forum enables teachers and parents to discuss High/Scope principles in more detail. Such discussions also help parents understand that the curriculum is based on solid child development information that can be applied in both the home and classroom settings. For example, in the "What Is Active Learning?" workshop, teachers explain the ingredients of active learning, then ask parents to list the ways their children are already actively involved at home. In addition, parents are encouraged to bring in a photo of their child engaging in active learning situations at home for teachers to display in the classroom. This gives teachers an opportunity to see the kinds of materials and activities children are interested in using at home and enables other parents to observe the variety of different choices children make in the home setting. In the workshop "Helping Children Resolve Social Conflicts," teachers share five strategies successfully used in the classroom to support children in conflict situations. Parents then have the option to use these proven strategies in common conflict situations their children face at home.

## Guiding Principles for Working With Adult Learners

High/Scope is committed to the principles of active learning and shared control in its work with both children and adults. Through our experience in designing workshops for parents, we have come to realize that the most effective workshops are those where staff and parents jointly contribute their knowledge and expertise to the discussions. In developing the workshop plans we have tried to strike a balance between offering parents sound child development information and providing plenty of opportunities for parents to present their own ideas and to discuss their individual experiences. Therefore, rather than convey information in lecture style, teachers employ a variety of strategies to encourage active parent participation. Some information is presented to the whole group with the aid of easy-to-follow charts and handouts; other activities occur in small groups or between partners to encourage parents to share ideas with one another and then with the whole group.

To support our philosophy of shared control, we have kept in mind the following three principles that constitute an "active learning" experience for parents: **supporting parents' construction of knowledge, facilitating teamwork,** and **encouraging follow-up.** It should be noted that we use the term *parents* throughout this book to refer to all adults who may attend parent workshops—extended family members, foster parents, friends, guardians, and any others who have an interest in learning and sharing more about the young children in their lives.

- **Supporting parents' construction of knowledge**—Adults, like children, benefit from considering and then relating new ideas to what they already know—from constructing their own knowledge in ways that are meaningful to them.

*Parents are often curious about what they see and hear in the High/Scope classroom. Workshops provide an opportunity for them to ask questions and to learn more about the High/Scope approach.*

When participating in the workshops presented in this book, parents and teachers alike will be actively engaged as they listen, speak, use relevant materials to better understand and explore ideas and strategies, and work together to solve problems related to specific issues. Parents will see, in concrete terms, how the information being shared can influence their current interactions with their children, and by understanding parents better, teachers will gain important insights into particular children's needs and interests. For example, in the workshop "Feeling Comfortable With Children's Social Bloopers," parents are asked to consider real-life scenarios, list the possible feelings they might experience in such situations, consider how they might react, and identify the message that reaction would send to their child. Teachers then lead a discussion about which reactions and messages parents feel might best benefit their child.

- **Facilitating teamwork**—Parenting is sometimes a daunting task. As parents gather together, they naturally will focus on their childrearing concerns—the difficulty of getting children ready for school or putting them to bed at night, the worry about whether their children will grow into successful and happy adults. To support and facilitate these types of exchanges, each workshop has time set aside for parents to share their childrearing dilemmas and successes. Teachers also offer their own experience and knowledge to guide parents to a deeper understanding of their children's growth and well-being. Participants can then work with one another to tackle tough issues of parenting within the framework of child development principles. For example, in the workshop "Transitions—Smooth Sailing or Daily Struggle?" parents break into small groups to identify common concerns related to transition times in their own households (waking up, going to school, going to bed) and consider a list of transition tips suggested by the teacher to support parents' efforts at home.

- **Encouraging follow-up**—After parents and teachers have had a chance to define problems, share experiences, and discuss solutions, parents need time and repeated opportunities to apply the information they have learned. Scheduling specific follow-up activities and establishing a two-way communication system will allow parents and teachers to be available to each other for support and discussion long past the actual meeting time. For instance, in the workshop "Cleaning, Shopping, Laundry, Home Repairs, Cooking, AND Playing With My Child?!" parents and teachers examine the educational value of having children and parents do chores together. For follow-up, teachers and parents put together prop boxes for parents to check out and use at home; these can be replenished and used long after the workshop has ended.

## How The Workshops Reflect the High/Scope Preschool Curriculum

The workshops have been designed to apply the principles of the High/Scope educational approach to situations parents face at home and in the community with their young children. The workshops are grouped in five major sections that reflect the five curriculum components identified in the High/Scope Preschool

"Wheel of Learning" (below): **active learning, daily routine, learning environment, adult-child interaction,** and **assessment.**

**The High/Scope Preschool "Wheel" of Learning**

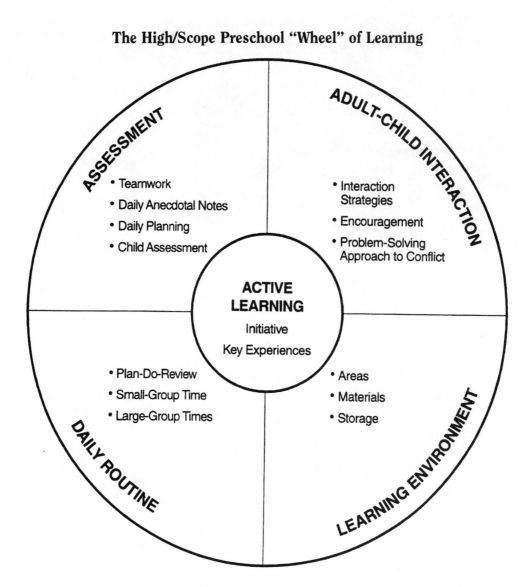

- **Active learning**—The center of the wheel reflects our firm belief that children learn best through **active experiences with materials, people, events, and ideas.** Active involvement and reflection on their experiences help children construct knowledge and make sense of the world around them. Young children are naturally curious. They like to explore new things, they ask questions and search for answers, and they try a variety of ways to solve the problems that come up as they pursue their ideas. This strong urge to take the initiative for learning and exploration leads children to engage in **key experiences,** important learning opportunities in ten key areas of development: *creative representation, language and literacy, initiative and social relations, movement, music, classification, seriation, number, space,* and

*Active learning is important not only for children but also for adults. Here, workshop participants explore a variety of materials in different ways to better understand the value of play and direct experience in early childhood education.*

*time.* (A complete list of the High/Scope preschool key experiences appears on pp. 36–37 as part of the workshop "Key Experiences—Promoting Mental, Emotional, Social, and Physical Growth.") The first section of the book, "Active Learning," contains workshops that explain the value of children as decision makers. Woven throughout this section is the philosophy that children will grow socially, emotionally, intellectually, and physically if given opportunities to interact with the people and materials around them. These workshops present sound child development information that will help parents better understand their children's behaviors and feelings.

- **Daily routine**—Children's emerging decision-making abilities are further supported by having a consistent **daily routine.** Being able to anticipate what happens next during the day gives children a certain amount of control over their everyday activities. The "Daily Routine" section of the wheel also reflects children's growing interest and skill in organizing their thoughts, following through on them, engaging in a process of reflection to review what happened, and then figuring out how to do things the same or differently the next time. The "Daily Routine" section of this book contains workshops that look at the way consistency in routines, combined with the active-learning philosophy, can actually simplify life for parents of young children. The workshops tackle common issues such as dealing with difficult transitions during the day, finding time to play with children while still getting housework done, and handling children's desire to follow through on their own intentions and ideas at home.

- **Learning environment**—For children to engage in key learning experiences in creative and purposeful ways, they need an accessible **learning environment** and appropriate materials to explore. Being able to independently find and return the materials they need to complete their plans will help encourage children to set realistic and attainable goals. Workshops in the "Learning Environment" section of this book help parents consider the importance to children's development of active physical play, the types of materials and toys offered to children, and the location and arrangement of those materials. For example, one workshop offers parents tips for providing toys that support children's learning; another offers practical strategies for reducing toy clutter at home.

- **Adult-child interaction**—Adults play an important role in helping children realize their goals. The "Adult-Child Interaction" section of the wheel focuses on how adults respond to children's initiatives and participate in their play so that children feel comfortable pursuing their own ideas. The "Adult-Child Interaction" section of this book explores ways in which children's unique personalities and individual strengths can be useful resources for adults to use in promoting and supporting positive interactions and communication. The child's increasing need for power and independence is discussed in this section, as well as a problem-solving approach to conflict that has long-term benefits for both children and adults.

- **Assessment**—The "Assessment" section of the High/Scope Preschool "Wheel of Learning" highlights the important role adults play in supporting and extending the young child's natural interest and excitement in constructing knowledge. It is our strong belief that parents as well as teachers—through careful child observation—can use what they see and hear children doing to guide their interactions with them and to plan ways to extend their experiences in appropriate ways. We labeled this last section of workshops "Special Topics" because it covers a variety of child observation issues that are relevant to both parents and teachers. The workshops focus attention on issues that impact families in everyday situations—for instance, traveling with children, sharing caregiving with other adults, and dealing with other people's negative reactions to children's behavior.

## How to Get the Most Out of the Workshops—Basic Presentation Tips

Conducting parent workshops can be intimidating to even the most seasoned classroom teacher. Facing a roomful of adults is very different from facing those parents' children in the familiar preschool setting. Following are some guidelines to consider when conducting parent meetings using the workshop plans that follow.

- **Do your homework well in advance of the meeting.** A simple poll of parental needs and interests will help you decide which of the 30 workshops presented here to include in your own workshop series. At the beginning of the school year, ask parents to choose the six topics they would most like to discuss during the school year. You may want to first review all 30 workshops to decide which two or three from each section you are most comfortable facilitating, and then send home a list of those workshops for parents to choose from. Once you have received parents' responses and identified the six workshops that seem to draw the most interest, make up a meeting schedule for the entire year. Send a calendar home to parents identifying the topic, date, and time of each workshop. Then be sure to announce the meetings again closer to the specific date—for example, put up posters and send reminder notices home. Also, invite each parent personally, and let them all know how important you think their participation is to the success of the meetings.

When you send home the initial list of workshop titles and any later announcements scheduling individual workshops, you may want to briefly explain the topics in a way that will interest your own group of parents. Here are some examples of how you might let parents know how a workshop will benefit them and their child personally:

| **Workshop title** | **Explanation** |
| --- | --- |
| #6—"Reading at Home" | *Choosing reading materials that will open your child's mind to new worlds and ideas* |
| #15—"Using Classroom Interest Areas as Keys to Gift Buying" | *Toys for your child that aren't advertised on TV* |
| #21—"Solving Everyday Problems: Opportunities for Learning" | *"Help me! My coat's upside down!" Helping children solve problems without taking over the task yourself* |
| #25—"Traveling With Children" | *"Are we there yet??" How you can make family travel enjoyable for you **and** your child* |

- **Make attending the meetings as convenient as possible for parents.** Parents are more likely to come to the workshops if they do not have to arrange and pay for babysitters, so offer child care in a nearby or adjoining space if workshops are held after school hours. Set out simple refreshments before parents arrive so that they can gather and mingle in a welcoming and informal atmosphere. As parents become more familiar with one another, you might help them arrange car pools or other kinds of shared transportation. (Other gatherings where parents and children participate with teachers are certainly encouraged within High/Scope's philosophy, but planning for those remains outside the scope of this book.)

- **As parents arrive for the meeting, greet them by name.** Place name tags and markers near the entranceway along with a sign asking parents to write their first name in large letters on the tag. Arrange seating so that parents gather

in groups of five to six each, and allow
5 minutes or so for informal conversation before beginning the workshop.
Round tables are ideal for this (in this
book the tables will be referred to as
"small-group tables"). As you begin,
be sure to thank everyone for coming!

*A classroom parent board is a convenient place to announce upcoming workshops and other events. It can also serve as a vehicle for parents to share some childrearing strategies and ideas with one another and with teachers.*

- **Be sensitive to the fact that parents may experience a range of feelings about attending the meeting.** Some parents might feel eager to attend and discuss childrearing issues with other parents and the teacher, while others might be disinterested in the topic but feel obliged to attend anyway. Some parents may even feel threatened by discussing personal issues and may worry that their own parenting style will be judged negatively by others. Be open and honest about these types of feelings if you think parents may be experiencing them or if *you* have some of your own. Acknowledge these feelings right from the beginning and as appropriate during the course of the workshops. A simple comment such as "This information is hard to tackle because it seems like there are no easy answers" can go a long way toward making everyone feel more at ease. The "Opening Activity" of each workshop is designed to get participants actively involved right away, so the sooner you get started with this, the less time parents will have to feel nervous or self-conscious about being at the meeting.

- **Remain flexible.** Use these workshop plans as a basis for your discussions, but tailor the language and the activities to fit the unique needs and interests of your group of parents. Add to the workshop content when you feel parents can absorb more information, or narrow the focus by discussing a single issue and giving parents more time to process information and plan follow-up ideas. Each workshop plan is designed to take approximately 1 hour; however, there are no hard and fast rules about how much time to allow for each section of the workshops. Keeping in mind your overall objectives for the workshop will help you decide which sections to focus on. Try not to spend too much time on any one activity during a workshop—be sure to leave enough time to bring the meeting to a close and for parents to make follow-up plans. As you move around the room during small-group activities, you may need to gently remind some groups to move along to the next part of the activity ("We have 3 minutes left until we discuss this with the whole group").

- **Clarify to parents in your initial survey, in the reminder announcements, and at the beginning of the workshop series that the workshops will be based on *active participation*.** Make it clear that you have an open-communication policy and that participants will have opportunities to solve problems and to discuss ways to adapt or generalize the information presented to their own situations. As parents work in pairs or small groups, circulate among them, listening, commenting, and referring parents to one another when appropriate. Answer questions parents might have for you, but also encourage them to problem solve together.

- **Be supportive of parents so they feel comfortable enough to want to share their own ideas with the group.** These workshops are not intended to be used to "fix" whatever presenters might feel parents are doing "wrong" at home. Make it clear that you are all there to share and to benefit from one another. Remind parents through your words, attitude, and actions that *they* are the experts on their children. Model acceptance, respect, and support for parents so that they feel comfortable, accept one another, and come to appreciate their own abilities to interact with their children in a similar manner. Provide an appropriate amount of information for your group, then focus on how to make parents feel successful and secure with the ideas. Avoid personal "How *I* solved this problem" stories, and keep your questions and comments focused on the *child,* not the parent. Gently lead parents to their own discoveries by asking focused yet open-ended questions. Avoid asking "why" questions, which tend to make people defensive or to bring the conversation to a halt. This type of question includes the following: *Why would you think she would like the same foods as you do? Have you ever considered how difficult that is for a 3-year-old child? Why do you think he would listen to you just because you said so?* Instead, ask "what" questions that offer open-ended options for parents, such as *What do you usually . . . ? What would happen if . . . ? Have you ever tried . . . ? What else might she have been trying to say to you when . . . ?* and *Help me to understand. . . .*

- **Do not act surprised or put off by parents who disagree with the information you share.** Giving participants an active role to play and a voice in the topic does not guarantee agreement and harmony—in fact, it might do quite the opposite simply because parents feel freer to share their feelings! Prior to the start of the workshop series, clearly state that your role as a presenter is to offer information about the topic being considered in relation to the educational approach you use with their children, and that their role is to react to and apply the ideas in ways that make sense to *them*. Acknowledge that you expect occasions when parents may not agree with the information shared by you or by other participants, but that you also expect the group will agree on some guidelines for handling lively debates and differences of opinion. Take a few minutes at the beginning of the workshop series to generate a list of guidelines that will allow all participants to comfortably exchange ideas and view issues from a new perspective. You may start the list for the group by putting two or three guidelines on a "Group Agreement List," then let parents add more ideas. Keep these posted for all subsequent workshops. Here are some ideas to help you get started: *Listen without interrupting until the other person is finished speaking. Agree to disagree on certain issues. Share what you feel comfortable sharing, and expect that the information will remain confidential.*

## Making It Happen—The Mechanics of the Workshop Plans

In each major section of the book, we offer 6 one-hour workshops for a total of 30 workshop plans. Each plan follows the same format:

- Goals
- Materials
- Introduction
- Opening Activity
- Central Ideas
- Reflections and Ideas for Application
- Follow-up Plans

   **Goals.** The ideas you hope to make parents aware of in a particular workshop are identified in the **goals** section. These simple statements give you an overall view of the purpose of the meeting and are not intended to be narrow, specific, measurable "objectives." For example, in the "Making Choices at Home" workshop, presenters learn that they will be discussing the choices that young children typically make at home, reasons for supporting these choices, and ways to balance children's needs to make choices with parents' need to set some guidelines for them.

   **Materials.** The **materials** section lists the supplies, including audio-visual equipment and handouts, you will need to collect prior to the workshop. When charts need to be created, the directions are set off in the text. Charts can be prepared either on large chart-pad paper on an easel or on an overhead transparency if you have a projector. All handouts for the workshops come after each individual workshop plan. You may make copies of the handouts for each participant; you might also want to make extras available for parents who are not able to attend the meetings. Occasionally, you will need to make photocopies of recommended articles or sections from other High/Scope publications.* These are referred to in the workshop material lists and also in the bibliography on p. 177. Optional resources mentioned throughout the workshops are presented at the end of this book.

**Introduction.** Whereas the goals section lists the reasons for the workshop for *your* benefit, the **introduction** rephrases them in everyday language for *parents*. You can use these statements to welcome parents to the workshop and to introduce the topic the group will be exploring and discussing. For example, in the introduction section of the "Making Choices at Home" workshop, the three simple goals are condensed into an even simpler introductory statement that lets parents know they will be focusing on the active learning ingredient of *choice* and how it relates to their children's everyday routine outside of school.

**Opening activity.** It is crucial to establish in the opening minutes of a session a climate in which participants will feel comfortable interacting and discussing issues and struggles that are often personal. The **opening activity** in each workshop serves this purpose. This activity focuses parents' attention on the topic in a nonthreatening and open-ended way. This short activity is designed to establish a rapport between you and the participants and to introduce the major theme or issue of the meeting. The major topic is often introduced during the "Opening Activity" from the viewpoint of the *parent* in order to set the stage for parents to understand how the issue affects their children. For example, during the "Traveling With Children" workshop, parents are asked to meet in small groups and describe to one another their positive memories about their own childhood vacations or travels. This nonthreatening discussion allows parents to construct their knowledge of travel from a *child's* perspective and encourages a feeling of camaraderie among group members.

**Central ideas.** The **central ideas** section lays out the major concepts and ideas of the workshop. You will use a variety of presentation techniques to actively engage parents. Through informational charts, small- and large-group discussions of scenarios, hands-on materials for demonstrating concepts, and handouts that inform and invite parents to apply the concepts in the home setting, parents gain a deeper understanding of the development of their own and other people's children. For instance, the "Seeing Children in a Positive Light" workshop gives parents the opportunity to experience firsthand the effect of negative labels upon one's behavior and then to replace common negative characterizations of *children's* behavior with descriptions that express a more positive view of the child. In most of the workshops, you will probably spend the bulk of

---

*Permission is granted from High/Scope Foundation to reprint up to 25 copies of handouts in this book or of material from other High/Scope publications mentioned in the workshops. Please contact High/Scope (phone 734-485-2000, ext. 298; fax 734-485-0704) to obtain permission to make more than 25 copies of material from High/Scope publications.

*As you talk with parents and listen to the issues that concern them, you may get ideas for additional workshops beyond the ones presented in this book.*

your meeting time discussing the central ideas.

**Reflections and ideas for application.** At this point in the workshop parents will have an opportunity to apply to daily situations that are concrete and realistic the general principles they have discussed. These situations may be actual experiences that parents relate or the true-to-life scenarios presented on the relevant charts and handouts. Many of these planned discussions encourage parents to work together as a team to support one another in their childrearing adventures. During the workshop "Understanding Children's Responsibilities Around the House," for instance, parents reflect together on parenting strategies that support or hinder children's attempts to take part in responsibilities at home. Parents then choose one supportive strategy to replace a hindering strategy they may consciously or unconsciously have been using at home.

**Follow-up plans.** Offering parents concise and practical ideas for applying the workshop information in their home setting is the goal of the **follow-up plans** section. We believe that the most effective workshops are those that end with a commitment on the part of the parents to somehow use and practice the information beyond the 1-hour meeting time. Some workshops call for parents to make an action plan to take home. For example, in the workshop "Rules—Set in Stone or Open to Family Discussion?" parents are asked to list rules they currently use in their own households, then choose two that they could rework based on the guidelines suggested during the workshop. In other cases, follow-up will involve displaying information in the classroom and/or having parents report back on strategies they have tried at home. Sometimes there are recommendations for books and videotapes you can make available in your parent lending library. The follow-up activity could also include plans for an additional workshop to further explore issues that arose during the meeting. As you bring each meeting to a close, remember to mention the time and topic of the next workshop and to invite parents to ask friends or extended family members to attend.

✳ ✳ ✳

In summary, our goal in this book is to provide a framework for early childhood classroom teachers and other professionals to use in a partnership with parents to facilitate the education of preschool-aged children. We remain committed to the idea that each adult has a valuable and unique perspective on children and that these perspectives, blended together, can aid both parents and professionals in discussing and solving problems connected with the emotional, physical, and intellectual health of children and families. It is in this spirit that we present *The Essential Parent Workshop Resource*.

# I.
# Active
# Learning

# What Is Active Learning?

## Goals

✔ To identify and define the five ingredients of active learning

✔ To discuss the role active learning plays in children's development

✔ To help parents identify ways in which they support their own children's active involvement at home

## Materials

- A poster displaying the five ingredients of active learning (materials, manipulation, choice, language from children, support from adults), illustrated with photos and samples of the children's work

- Materials for making name tags: colored paper, scissors, hole punchers, string, markers, glitter glue

- Several small brown bags

- Blank stick-on name tags and several black markers

- Chart pad and markers or overhead projector

- Chart 1A (prepared ahead of time on a large piece of chart paper or an overhead transparency)

- Handouts: "Positive Outcomes of Active Learning"
  "The Ingredients and Process of Active Learning"

## Introduction

1. Greet parents by name as they arrive. Tell them that the topic for the meeting tonight will be active learning, and invite them to look at the display illustrating the five ingredients.

2. After 5 minutes of informal conversation, have parents gather in small groups of four to five each.

## Opening Activity

3. Pass out a prepared bag of name-tag-making materials to half of the small groups and blank tags and one black marker (per group) to the other half. Ask

parents in the first group to design, in any way they'd like, their own name tags. Instruct the other groups to share the black marker and write their first names only in capital letters on the blank tags, then to peel off the stickers and place the tags on their clothing just under their left shoulder.

4. Give parents about 10 minutes to complete their name tags. Ask the groups that are not designing their own tags to simply wait quietly. When there are 2 minutes left, let parents know that it is almost time to clean up their materials.

### Central Ideas

5. Using Chart 1A, "Ingredients of Active Learning," read the definition of active learning and ask parents to keep it in mind as you reflect together on the name-tag activity. Go through each of the five ingredients and record concrete examples from the groups that designed their own name tags. Then do the same for the parents who were instructed on how to make their tags, and discuss what ingredients these groups missed out on. For example, your chart might look like this:

**Chart 1A—Use in Step #5**
INGREDIENTS OF ACTIVE LEARNING

Children learn about the world around them by interacting with materials, people, events, and ideas. This process is called active learning.

**Groups designing own tags**
- MANIPULATION:
- MATERIALS:
- CHOICE:
- LANGUAGE FROM CHILDREN:
- SUPPORT FROM ADULTS:

**Groups instructed by leader**
- MANIPULATION:
- MATERIALS:
- CHOICE:
- LANGUAGE FROM CHILDREN:
- SUPPORT FROM ADULTS:

## Groups designing own tags

- **Materials**—paper, scissors, hole punchers, string, markers, glitter glue
- **Manipulation**—squeezing, cutting, tearing, designing
- **Choice**—some names written in glitter, others with markers; some attached to necks, others folded and placed in front of person at table
- **Language**—conversation about the latest flu bug going around, a vacation trip coming up, other occasions when parents have had a chance to use art materials
- **Support**—holding a string for someone else to cut, sufficient time and a variety of interesting materials provided

## Groups instructed by leader

- **Materials**—(limited) marker and tags
- **Manipulation**—(limited) writing name, peeling and sticking tag to clothing
- **Choice**—(limited) slight variation in letter design and size
- **Language**—conversation about who their children are, comments about why other groups get to make their own tags

- **Support**—(limited) specific directions, few materials, long waiting time

6. Explain that active learning forms the basis of this curriculum and that the classroom staff believes in its positive social and educational outcomes for children. Pass out the handout "Positive Outcomes of Active Learning" and invite comments and questions from parents. When you discuss the third point on the handout *(maintain interest and minimize boredom)*, remind parents how boring it must have been for the groups that did not get to design their own tag during the opening activity, and relate this to how children often feel when they are asked to be passive in similar situations.

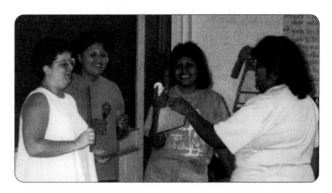

*The importance of active learning is brought home to parents when they experience it for themselves!*

## Reflections and Ideas for Application

7. Make a list of ways parents notice and support their own children's active involvement at home. Examples might include such things as *picks out own clothing in the morning, chooses bedtime story, puts the plates on the table for dinner, plays in mud puddle with bare feet, squeezes toothpaste onto the toothbrush.*

8. Review the concept of active learning using the handout titled "The Ingredients and Process of Active Learning." Explain to parents that in future meetings you will continue to examine these active learning ingredients and the ways they impact their children's educational experiences.

9. Explain to parents the format for future meetings: each will include goals for the meeting, an opening activity to introduce the topic, small- and large-group discussions about the main ideas, and a time to reflect on ways the information presented can be used at home.

10. Thank parents for coming and ask them to bring a photograph to add to the classroom of their child playing at home or going on a family outing.

## Follow-up Plans

11. Hang the photos parents bring in where children can see them. If possible, place them near the entranceway so families can enjoy them together.

12. Highlight the ingredients of active learning by displaying the variety of ways children use the same materials. In conversations with parents, emphasize the ways the materials are meaningful and unique to their children by commenting on what you saw them do or heard them say while using the materials.

13. Provide a copy of the videotape "Supporting Children's Active Learning: Teaching Strategies for Diverse Settings" for parents to check out in the parent lending library (available from High/Scope Press—see p. 182).

**HANDOUT**

# Positive Outcomes of Active Learning

- Provides opportunities for children and adults to invent and discover together by exploring materials and ideas and by experiencing events
- Minimizes adult-child conflict by encouraging adults to support and extend children's **own** choices, ideas, and efforts
- Helps children maintain interest in the learning process and minimizes boredom by allowing them to do what is important to *them*
- Provides opportunities for children to develop the skills to take care of their own needs and solve their own problems

***Discussion notes:***

**HANDOUT**

# The Ingredients and Process of Active Learning

## What are the ingredients of active learning?

An active learning experience includes the following five ingredients:

- **Materials.** Children explore and play with objects that they find appealing and interesting. The best materials for learning are those that children can use in a variety of ways.

- **Manipulation.** Children explore and combine materials in a direct, hands-on, physical way.

- **Choice.** Children have the opportunity to choose for themselves what to do with materials.

- **Language from children.** Children use language to describe what they are doing.

- **Support from adults.** Adults encourage, assist, and participate in children's activities.

## What is the active learning process?

### *Physical activity*

Children use their **whole bodies** and **all their senses** to explore and learn about objects. Some of the active, physical ways preschool children use materials include pushing, pulling, squeezing, tapping, taking apart, putting together, squishing, smelling, licking, shaking, rolling, and pounding. Through these experiences children construct an understanding of the objects around them: *balls roll, water splashes, ice is cold and slippery, carrot sticks taste better than pencils.*

### *Mental activity*

As children explore materials and ideas, they are also **mentally active.** They initiate their own plans. Their interactions are thoughtful: they ask and answer their own questions, and they encounter and solve problems as they work with materials. This process of planning, testing, questioning, and experimenting helps children develop a better understanding of the world. Here are some examples of the questions children consider as they work with materials: *Which ball will roll faster? How can I get the roof to stay on my block house? What can I use to make my sister a birthday card?*

This combination of mental and physical activity is what we call **active learning.** When the ingredients of active learning are present, children develop and grow as thinkers, learners, and doers.

# 2 Making Choices at Home

### Goals

✔ To examine choices that children naturally make at home
✔ To discuss the reasons for supporting children's choices at home and the impact these choices have on parents
✔ To look at ways to balance children's and parents' needs

### Materials

- Handouts: "Children as Choice Makers"
              "Looking for a Balance"
- Large piece of chart paper with two columns labeled "Choices I'm Comfortable With" and "Choices I'm Not Comfortable With"

### Introduction

1. Begin by telling parents that the meeting will focus on the active learning ingredient **choice** as it relates to their children's everyday routine outside of school.

### Opening Activity

2. Pass out the handout titled "Children as Choice Makers." Ask parents to break up into groups of four or five each and follow the directions written on the top of the handout. Give them about 15 minutes to complete this activity.

### Central Ideas

3. Meet back as a whole group. Using their small-group examples as a guide, lead a discussion about the value of giving children choices in their everyday routines. Talk specifically about what parents feel are acceptable choices, and record several of their responses in the appropriate columns on the chart paper. For example, under the "Choices I'm Comfortable With" column, you might write *choosing cooked or raw carrots for lunch;* under the "Choices I'm *Not* Comfortable With" column, you might write *watching violent videos* or

*playing with war toys.* Be sure to acknowledge parents' answers as you record them: "Eating vegetables *is* essential for children's health." "Violence is an ever-present concern."

## Reflections and Ideas for Application

4. Pass out the handout "Looking for a Balance." Do *Scenario One* together, then ask parents to complete the handout in small groups. Allow about 10 minutes for them to finish.

5. Meet back as a large group and highlight some of the discussed solutions. Focus particularly on the ideas parents suggest for ways to give children choices even in "non-negotiable" situations (for example, giving a child a choice of three flavors of toothpaste while enforcing the tooth-brushing-before-bed routine).

## Follow-up Plans

6. Display pictures of children making choices in the classroom. Include activities like working at the computer, playing house and dressing up, painting a picture, or looking for bugs with a magnifying glass.

**HANDOUT**

# Children as Choice Makers

Use the list below to talk about the kinds of choices and decisions you see your own children making (or wanting to make) during their everyday routines. For example, you may have a child who always wants to wear sweatpants to school or whose food preferences include anything with cheese on it.

*Clothes:*

*Food:*

*Television programs, computer games, or books:*

*Toys or games:*

*Friends or family members they play with:*

*Other choices to add:*

**HANDOUT**

# Looking for a Balance

Sometimes the choices children make clash with your own values or wishes as parents. Below are three strategies you can use when you don't agree with children's choices. For each scenario that follows, write three solutions—one to correspond with each strategy presented. Discuss which solution you might prefer in each case.

### Strategy #1

Decide which battles are most important to fight. Ignore the others.

### Strategy #2

Give an honest and accurate reason for challenging the child's choice.

### Strategy #3

Offer a similar alternative.

### Scenario One

EVEN IN THE HOT SUMMER MONTHS, YOUR DAUGHTER ASKS TO WEAR LONG-SLEEVED SHIRTS.

#1: LET HER; IF SHE GETS HOT SHE'LL PROBABLY ASK TO CHANGE.

#2: TELL HER "SHORT SLEEVES ARE BETTER WHEN IT'S HOT LIKE THIS. I'M WORRIED YOU'LL GET TOO HOT IN LONG SLEEVES AND FEEL SICK."

#3: OFFER LONG-SLEEVED SHIRTS IN LIGHT COLORS AND LIGHTWEIGHT FABRICS.

### Scenario Two

Your child only eats pizza, macaroni and cheese, and French fries.

#1:

●●●▶

#2:

#3:

## Scenario Three

The games, toys, and television shows your child likes are often violent and involve weapons like guns and swords.

#1:

#2:

#3:

*Your own scenarios:*

# 3 Math in the Preschool Years

## Goals

✔ To examine the differences between children's and adults' thinking about number concepts

✔ To expand parents' idea of what *number* means

✔ To look at how children's understanding of *number* changes over time

✔ To generate ideas for parents to actively support children's curiosity about *number* at home

## Materials

- Handouts: "Young Children and Numbers"
  "Preschoolers' Understanding of *Number*"
  "Support Strategies to Strengthen Children's Understanding of Number Concepts"
- Pencils and pens for each small group of parents

## Introduction

1. Explain to parents that you would like to explore what "math" means to preschool children and to offer ways for parents to support children's understanding of number concepts.

## Opening Activity

2. Pass out the handout titled "Young Children and Numbers." Ask parents to read the scenarios and, with two or three other parents, discuss how the children in the anecdotes understand the concept of *number* differently than adults might. Give parents 10 minutes to read and react to the scenarios.

3. Gather back together and ask parents to comment on the scenarios.

## Central Ideas

4. Using the handout "Preschoolers' Understanding of *Number*" as a guide, discuss from a developmental perspective children's understanding of number.

Have parents break up into small groups, and assign each group a numbered item from the handout. Ask them to read and discuss their item and prepare a brief summary of the item to share with the other groups.

5. Meet back as a large group and ask a spokesperson from each group to share the group's summary and comments. For each point on the handout, encourage parents from other groups to ask questions, make comments, or share anecdotes from their own experience. Be sure to highlight—if parents do not—the point about not correcting children's counting inaccuracies.

## Reflections and Ideas for Application

6. Explain to parents that children's understanding of number develops over time and with experience, and adults can use support strategies during everyday experiences that will help build the foundation for this development. Have parents break up into small groups again, and pass out the discussion sheet titled "Support Strategies to Strengthen Children's Understanding of Number Concepts." Ask the groups to complete the sheet following the directions as written.

7. As a whole group, summarize the additional examples of support strategies generated by the smaller groups. Ask parents to try one of the suggested strategies at home over the next week and record their child's reactions, either in writing or in a conversation with you.

## Follow-up Plans

8. Collect the anecdotes that parents relate to you in Step #7. Write and post them on a parent bulletin board titled "Children and Numbers."

*Children develop an understanding of number concepts as they play with materials, act out experiences, and talk to interested adults. This child is exploring patterns using plastic animals and blocks.*

**HANDOUT**

# Young Children and Numbers

Read the following stories about preschool-aged children and their everyday experiences with math. Talk with the members of your group about the ways the child's thinking in the scenario differs from that of an older child or an adult. The first story has the comment section already filled out. As a group, fill out the comment section for the remaining scenarios.

### Scenario One

You take your 3- and 6-year-old children trick-or-treating. Upon their return they dump their candy out on the kitchen floor. Suddenly you hear your 3-year-old child screaming, "Sister has more!" You notice that it looks like your older child has more candy because she has spread it out in a long row instead of putting it all in a pile.

*Comment:*

MOST 6-YEAR-OLD CHILDREN CAN UNDERSTAND THAT ALTHOUGH SPREADING THE CANDY OVER A LARGER SPACE MAKES IT LOOK LIKE MORE, THE AMOUNT ACTUALLY STAYS THE SAME NO MATTER HOW IT IS ARRANGED. A 3-YEAR-OLD CHILD, ON THE OTHER HAND, IS GUIDED BY APPEARANCES: IF IT LOOKS LIKE MORE, THEN IT MUST BE MORE.

### Scenario Two

You are outside digging in the soil for a bulb garden with your 4-year-old daughter who says, "Look, Mom, I have a whole lot of earthworms." Although there are only 6, she counts 10, touching some of them twice as she counts.

*Comment:*

•••▶

## Scenario Three

You ask your 4-year-old son to help you set the table for dinner. When he is done you notice that some plates have two forks, others have one, and some have only spoons next to them.

*Comment:*

# Preschoolers' Understanding of *Number*

1. **Young children spontaneously collect items and put things into groups.** They still judge amount by appearance, so they will often be inaccurate when comparing the number of items in a group, especially if the numbers are large. Their collections need not be of fancy store-bought materials. Children are quite happy to collect and group everyday objects like rocks, stones, pebbles, buttons, leaves, Cheerios, and dandelions.

2. **When children count objects, it is common for them to use some number names in the correct order and some number names in an unconventional order.** For example, a young child might say, "1, 2, 3, 4, 5, 6, 7, 8, 9, 10, 11, 12, 14, 13, 10." At this age, the *process* of counting and the pleasure it gives children are much more important than counting in the correct order. Resist the urge to correct children as doing so may actually discourage them from counting in the way that makes sense to them right now. Young children can and should see counting as something fun, not as a test. With practice and experience—counting street lights, the candles on a pretend birthday cake, the eyes on your face, the freckles on your arms, the cars in a parking lot, the wheels on a truck—children *will* learn to count without being drilled by adults.

3. **As children play, you will see them spontaneously arranging items in one-to-one correspondence:** two chairs "for the two people driving their car to the grocery store," a hat for each of the dolls, or one stone inside each compartment of an ice cube tray. Again, children will sometimes be accurate in these one-to-one relationships; at other times, they might put two spoons next to one plate. Once again, encourage and support their *efforts* rather than focusing on *accuracy*.

**HANDOUT**

# Support Strategies to Strengthen Children's Understanding of Number Concepts

Consider the support strategy suggestions below and add examples under each—things that you have heard your own children say or ideas that you would like to try in your own interactions with them.

### Strategy #1

**Listen to and accept the ways children describe and compare amounts or the number of objects.**

*"YOUR DRESS HAS MORE BUTTONS 'CAUSE THEY'RE BIGGER."*

*"I'M MAKING A TON OF PANCAKES, SO I CAN'T BE HUNGRY."*

*"SHE HAS MORE CANDLES ON HER CAKE THAN MINE."*

*Other examples:*

### Strategy #2

**Use words like *more*, *fewer*, and *the same number* in everyday conversations with children.**

*"I SEE YOU PUT MORE BEADS ON THIS STRING THAN YOU PUT ON THAT ONE."*

*"YOU CHOSE THE SAME NUMBER OF CRACKERS I DID."*

*"LOOK, THERE ARE FEWER BUTTONS ON YOUR COAT THAN THERE ARE ON YOUR JACKET."*

*Other examples:*

•••▶

## Strategy #3

Capitalize on children's natural interest in counting objects.

COUNT THE NUMBER OF STEPS TO GET TO THE BEDROOM AT BEDTIME.

COUNT THE NUMBER OF GROCERY ITEMS YOU PUT IN THE CART OR ON THE COUNTER.

COUNT THE NUMBER OF PUSHES YOU GIVE YOUR CHILD ON A SWING.

*Other examples:*

## Strategy #4

Give children opportunities to experience one-to-one correspondence.

ENCOURAGE YOUR SON TO PUT ONE LID BACK ON EACH MARKER HE COLORS WITH.

ASK YOUR CHILD TO FIND THE LIDS THAT WILL FIT ON DIFFERENT LEFTOVER FOOD STORAGE CONTAINERS.

MAKE A GAME WITH EMPTY EGG CARTONS AND PLASTIC EGGS.

*Other examples:*

# Key Experiences— Promoting Mental, Emotional, Social, and Physical Growth

## Goals

✔ To familiarize parents with the list of 58 key experiences

✔ To explain that key experiences occur naturally and act as a guide for adult thinking and understanding when they observe and interact with children

## Materials

- Definition of key experiences written on a large piece of chart paper or an overhead transparency: *Key Experiences—a description of what young children do as they interact with the people and materials around them, how they look at the world, and the kinds of experiences that are important for their development*
- Play dough (enough for everyone to have a chunk)
- Plastic straws of various widths and lengths
- Key experience handout
- An assortment of photographs taken of the children during class time. Each child from the class should be in at least one of the photos, all key experience areas should be represented, and photos should be accompanied by captions that describe what is happening in the picture. Use direct quotes from the children involved whenever appropriate.

## Introduction

1. Tell parents that the topic of the meeting will be the key experiences. Explain that the key experiences serve classroom staff as a guide for observing children and planning a stimulating learning environment for them and will be used during conference times to share information with parents about their own children. Share the definition of key experiences that you have written on the chart paper or overhead transparency.

## Opening Activity

2. Have parents divide into groups of four to five each. Pass out a chunk of play dough and several straw sections to each parent. Tell parents they have 10

minutes to play with the play dough and straw sections, using them in any way they like. Emphasize that they can work alone or with others at their table. Set aside a table in the room for parents to display their work if they choose.

## Central Ideas

3. After 10 minutes, pass out the key experience handout. Assign one half of the tables the key experiences in creative representation, language and literacy, initiative and social relations, movement, and music. Assign the other half of the tables the classification, seriation, number, space, and time key experiences.

4. Have parents in each group identify from their assigned lists the key experiences that reflect their own actions and words during the earlier play dough activity. Ask them to choose one key experience and supporting anecdote to share with the entire group. Some examples: rolling the play dough into a long, thin piece—*changing the shape and arrangement of objects;* making a play dough "cake" with straw "candles"—*making models out of clay and other materials;* lining up straw sections by size—*arranging several things one after another in a series.*

5. Once each table has reported to the whole group, point out that key experiences are **not taught** but rather grow out of direct experiences with people, materials, ideas, and events. Explain that, just as they observed for themselves in their play dough activity, key experiences occur naturally when children are given the opportunity to initiate their own activities and use materials in ways that make sense to them. Point out that the key experiences also describe the social, emotional, cognitive, and physical development of children from the ages of 2½ to 5.

## Reflections and Ideas for Application

6. Pass out the photographs taken of the parents' children during the course of the school day. Ask the small groups to look for examples of key experiences represented in the photos, focusing on the key experience categories that they did not focus on in Step #4. Have each group again share one example with the entire group.

7. Before ending the meeting, ask parents to discuss ways they can use at home the information they have learned about key experiences. To guide this process, have them complete the following sentences in their small groups.
   • *My child already takes care of his or her own needs by . . .*
   • *Another initiative and social relations key experience I will watch for is . . .*

## Follow-up Plans

8. Display the photos of the children on a classroom bulletin board. Group the pictures according to the key experience categories.

*Photographs of children participating in a variety of key experiences can help parents recognize how natural this process is for children. Here, children are making models out of materials (creative representation) and taking care of their own needs (initiative and social relations).*

9.  Display the key experiences on the board. (The Preschool Key Experience Posters, Key Experience Chart, and Wheel of Learning/Key Experience card are all available from High/Scope Press—see p. 182.)

10. Ask for a parent volunteer to take additional photos of the children in the classroom as they initiate their own activities. Add these pictures to the key experience bulletin board.

11. Solicit anecdotes from parents to add to the board.

# High/Scope Preschool Key Experiences

## Creative Representation

- Recognizing objects by sight, sound, touch, taste, and smell
- Imitating actions and sounds
- Relating models, pictures, and photographs to real places and things
- Pretending and role playing
- Making models out of clay, blocks, and other materials
- Drawing and painting

## Language and Literacy

- Talking with others about personally meaningful experiences
- Describing objects, events, and relations
- Having fun with language: listening to stories and poems, making up stories and rhymes
- Writing in various ways: drawing, scribbling, letterlike forms, invented spelling, conventional forms
- Reading in various ways: reading storybooks, signs and symbols, one's own writing
- Dictating stories

## Initiative and Social Relations

- Making and expressing choices, plans, and decisions
- Solving problems encountered in play
- Taking care of one's own needs
- Expressing feelings in words
- Participating in group routines
- Being sensitive to the feelings, interests, and needs of others
- Building relationships with children and adults
- Creating and experiencing collaborative play
- Dealing with social conflict

## Movement

- Moving in nonlocomotor ways (anchored movement: bending, twisting, rocking, swinging one's arms)
- Moving in locomotor ways (non-anchored movement: running, jumping, hopping, skipping, marching, climbing)
- Moving with objects
- Expressing creativity in movement
- Describing movement
- Acting upon movement directions
- Feeling and expressing steady beat
- Moving in sequences to a common beat

•• ● ▶

## Music
- Moving to music
- Exploring and identifying sounds
- Exploring the singing voice
- Developing melody
- Singing songs
- Playing simple musical instruments

## Classification
- Exploring and describing similarities, differences, and the attributes of things
- Distinguishing and describing shapes
- Sorting and matching
- Using and describing something in several ways
- Holding more than one attribute in mind at a time
- Distinguishing between "some" and "all"
- Describing characteristics something does not possess or what class it does not belong to

## Seriation
- Comparing attributes (longer/shorter, bigger/smaller)
- Arranging several things one after another in a series or pattern and describing the relationships (big/bigger/biggest, red/blue/red/blue)
- Fitting one ordered set of objects to another through trial and error (small cup–small saucer/medium cup–medium saucer/big cup–big saucer)

## Number
- Comparing the numbers of things in two sets to determine "more," "fewer," "same number"
- Arranging two sets of objects in one-to-one correspondence
- Counting objects

## Space
- Filling and emptying
- Fitting things together and taking them apart
- Changing the shape and arrangement of objects (wrapping, twisting, stretching, stacking, enclosing)
- Observing people, places, and things from different spatial viewpoints
- Experiencing and describing positions, directions, and distances in the play space, building, and neighborhood
- Interpreting spatial relations in drawings, pictures, and photographs

## Time
- Starting and stopping an action on signal
- Experiencing and describing rates of movement
- Experiencing and comparing time intervals
- Anticipating, remembering, and describing sequences of events

# How Many Days Until...? Anticipating Special Events With Children

## Goals

✔ To examine young children's understanding of the concept of time

✔ To look at concrete ways adults can support children's understanding of time

✔ To generate strategies adults can use to help children prepare for upcoming special events

## Materials

- Handouts: "Opening Activity Worksheet"
        "Tips for Celebrating the Coming of Special Events With Children"
- Chart pad and markers or overhead projector
- Chart 5A (prepared ahead of time on a large piece of chart paper or an overhead transparency)
- Several copies* of the article "Celebrating With Preschoolers" (Susan M. Terdan, *Supporting Young Learners 2: Ideas for Child Care Providers and Teachers,* 1996, pp. 247–254)

## Introduction

1. Tell parents that you will be examining the differences between adults' and young children's understanding of time. Together you will also brainstorm ways that parents can support their children as they look forward to special family events like holiday celebrations, birthdays, or family vacations.

## Opening Activity

2. Ask parents to choose a partner, either another adult attending with them or one of the other parents. Give each pair a copy of the "Opening Activity Worksheet." Ask them to follow the directions written on the handout.

---

*Please see p. 12 for information on copying High/Scope publications.

## Central Ideas

3. After a few moments, engage the whole group in discussing how confusing and impossible the opening activity task was. Explain that this activity simulates "calendar time" for children, and relate parents' reactions to the confusion young children feel when asked to interpret clocks or calendars. Together, generate a list of **concrete** ways people know what event or activity is next without using a clock or calendar. Start the list on a sheet of chart paper or on an overhead transparency with ideas such as *taking a bath and putting on pajamas, your stomach rumbling, the sun rising or setting.* Point out that children can successfully use *these* types of aids—rather than conventional aids like clocks or calendars—to gauge the passage of time and the coming of events.

**Chart 5A—Use in Step #4**
TIME LIMITATIONS

- YOUNG CHILDREN OFTEN HAVE A HARD TIME THINKING FAR INTO THE FUTURE OR REFLECTING ON EVENTS THAT ARE LONG PAST.

- CONVENTIONAL TIME UNITS LIKE WEEKS, MONTHS, AND YEARS ARE *NOT* MEANINGFUL TO YOUNG CHILDREN.

- NOTHING IS MORE RELEVANT TO YOUNG CHILDREN THAN WHAT THEY ARE DOING RIGHT NOW.

4. Share with parents the information about young children's understanding of time concepts and special occasions on Chart 5A. Cite an example or two for each point, and ask parents to add observations from their own experience.

## Reflections and Ideas for Application

5. Give each parent a copy of the handout titled "Tips for Celebrating the Coming of Special Events With Children." Review each point on the handout together.

6. Have parents break into groups of three or four, and give each group a large sheet of chart paper and a marker. Have each group write down a special occasion commonly celebrated in their families. Next, ask them to list **concrete** ways children understand the occasion is coming. Then, using the five suggestions on the "Tips for Celebrating Special Events" handout as a guide, have them come up with additional ways to help children anticipate the holiday or special occasion they have chosen.

7. Hang parents' lists around the room. Let them walk around and read each one, marking any items for which they want further information or clarification.

8. Together discuss those points that parents want further information about, asking the originators of each point to address the questions.

**Follow-up Plans**

9. Pass out a copy of the article "Celebrating With Preschoolers" to each family attending the meeting. Make additional copies available for those who were not in attendance.

10. From the lists created by parents in Step #6, summarize the special events and concrete suggestions they identified. Post this summary on the parent bulletin board.

**HANDOUT**

# Opening Activity Worksheet

In the space provided below, make a to-do list of all the ways you'll have to prepare for these upcoming events. Include extra items you might need to buy at the grocery store, dates when you will need to notify people, and appointments you will need to make.

| モュソリヲキキ | | | | | | |
|---|---|---|---|---|---|---|
| ‼ | | ₵ | | | | |
| | | | | | ♣ | |
| | ⊠ | | ⚙ | | | |
| ⚙ | | | | ❦ | | ✳ |

# Tips for Celebrating the Coming of Special Events With Children

1. **Provide experiences that will spark your child's natural curiosity about upcoming events and special occasions.** Some examples include walking through a downtown area or neighborhood to look at holiday decorations and window displays, looking at photos of vacation trips you have taken, going to the store to pick out party decorations, and planning a menu together for an upcoming special meal.

2. **Establish traditions that will help your child anticipate an upcoming event.** For example, take a trip to a pumpkin patch or make masks for Halloween; go to a cake-decorating shop to pick out decorations for the top of a birthday cake.

3. **Use concrete ways to help children mark the days until a special event.** Using words like "Your birthday is after three more nights' sleep" is more understandable to a child than "Your birthday is on June 7." To help prepare a child for a special visit to Grandma's house, you could blow up 5 balloons 5 days ahead of time and have your child pop 1 balloon a day for the "countdown." Or, you could put out 5 apples and share one each day.

4. **Watch and listen carefully to your child for clues about his or her understanding of an approaching or past holiday.** If your son makes scribbles or letters on paper and tells you it's a Valentine for his teacher, you have a starting place for extending your child's understanding of this holiday.

5. **Expect and plan for children to celebrate a holiday long past its official date on the calendar.** Offer appropriate materials and interact with children as they re-enact, for instance, cutting down and decorating the Christmas tree, lighting the Hanukkah candles, or dressing up in costume. Supporting children's interest in holidays both before and afterwards will help them understand these occasions better.

# 6 Getting Beyond "What Did You Do at School Today?"

## Goals

✔ To consider basic principles of language and how children develop conversational skills

✔ To practice a conversational technique that encourages children to talk about things that are of interest and importance to them

## Materials

- Chart pad and markers or overhead projector
- Charts 6A and 6B (prepared ahead of time on a large piece of chart paper or an overhead transparency)
- Handout titled "Child Contributions and Adult Acknowledgments in Conversation"

## Introduction

1. Encourage parents to talk to one another informally for a few minutes before you begin the workshop.

2. Tell parents that tonight you will be sharing information about why it is important to have conversations with young children. Explain that you will be practicing a conversational technique that encourages children to talk about things that are important to them and that lets them know you value what they say.

## Opening Activity

3. Ask parents to think back to the conversations they have just engaged in or to another recent conversation with an adult. Have them share the thoughts and feelings they experienced during these conversations. Parents might share things such as "She seemed interested in what I was saying." "It gave me a chance to know him better." "It was nice to talk to another adult after being at home with my children all day!"

4. In groups of three or four, ask parents to discuss the things they do (consciously or unconsciously) while talking to another adult that gives both speakers a chance to say things that are important to them. As a whole group, discuss these strategies and write them on a large piece of chart paper or an overhead transparency. Answers might include *make eye contact, listen without interrupting, ask about something you know is going on in the other person's life.*

## Central Ideas

5. Explain to parents that although adults usually share control of conversations through means such as those just discussed, adults often talk to *children* in ways that give children little choice in the conversation. For instance, we ask them closed questions with just one right answer, or we bring up a conversation that has little to do with what the child is focused on at that moment. Explain that the next activity will highlight three conversational strategies often used with children that give control mostly to the adult, as well as one strategy that gives children the opportunity to express their own interests.

6. With the whole group, discuss the strategies listed on Chart 6A, "Conversational Moves." For *each* conversational move, first review the definition. Next, ask for a parent volunteer to role-play your conversational partner (suggested scripts are below). Finally, ask parents to find a partner and practice that conversational move using their own examples. Do each of these three steps before moving on to the next conversational move.

Scripts for role-playing may go like this:

**Chart 6A—Use in Step #6**
CONVERSATIONAL MOVES

• MOVE #1: ENFORCED REPETITION—TELLING THE OTHER PERSON WHAT TO SAY

• MOVE #2: CLOSED QUESTIONS—ASKING QUESTIONS THAT HAVE ONLY ONE RIGHT ANSWER

• MOVE #3: OPEN QUESTIONS—ASKING QUESTIONS THAT COULD HAVE MANY DIFFERENT ANSWERS (ON A TOPIC YOU CHOOSE), FOLLOWING EACH QUESTION WITH ANOTHER

• MOVE #4: CONTRIBUTIONS AND ACKNOWLEDGMENTS—OBSERVATIONS AND STATEMENTS THE OTHER PERSON INITIATES FOLLOWED BY A WORD, PHRASE, OR GESTURE YOU MAKE TO LET THE OTHER PERSON KNOW YOU ARE LISTENING

- **Move #1: Enforced repetition.** Direct your partner to say something to another parent: *"Joan, tell Paul that you like his shirt." "Lars, tell Christine 'Thank you' for making room at the table for you."*

- **Move #2: Closed questions.** Ask your partner a series of one-answer questions, pausing a moment in between for an answer: *"Ann Marie, how many children do you have? What are their ages? When are their birthdays?"*

- **Move #3: Open questions.** Ask your partner questions that could be answered in a number of different ways. After your partner responds, ask another question: *"Shawna, Terrell told the class you got a new puppy. How has your family reacted to him? How are you going to train him?"*

- **Move #4: Contributions and acknowledgments.** After the speaker makes an observation or statement, follow this contribution with a word, phrase, or gesture that lets the speaker know you are listening: *Presenter: "I appreciate the time you made to come to the meeting tonight." Participant: "Yeah, we had to eat in a hurry before coming." Presenter: "It's hard to squeeze everything in that needs to get done."*

7. To summarize, ask the group to comment on how it feels to be talked to in each of these ways. Answers may include "I feel put on the spot and talked down to." "There isn't much chance for the other person to say anything else." "It seems bossy to ask so many questions." "I feel like he really heard me." For each conversational move, have parents generate one or two examples that adults typically use with children. For example, *"Say 'Thank you' for the lovely birthday present." "How old are you?" "Did you have fun at school today?"* Discuss the way each of these strategies might limit or encourage conversations between children and adults. For instance, although open questions allow children to respond in a variety of ways, they are usually centered on topics *adults* are interested in rather than topics of children's choosing.

## Reflections and Ideas for Application

8. With the whole group, discuss the basic language principles written on Chart 6B. Connect these principles to the points parents made in Step #7.

9. To help parents better understand the conversational techniques of contributions and acknowledgments, pass out the handout titled "Child Contributions and Adult Acknowledgments in Conversation." Have parents divide into groups of three or four and follow the directions stated on the handout. Meet back as a whole group and respond to comments or questions. Point out the way the sample adult acknowledgments leave plenty of room for children to respond as they choose.

## Follow-up Plans

10. Ask parents to practice, before the next meeting, acknowledging the contributions their children and

> **Chart 6B—Use in Step #8**
> BASIC LANGUAGE PRINCIPLES
>
> - LANGUAGE HELPS US ESTABLISH AND MAINTAIN RELATIONSHIPS WITH OTHERS.
>
> - CHILDREN WANT TO COMMUNICATE, TO UNDERSTAND, AND TO BE UNDERSTOOD.
>
> - LANGUAGE NATURALLY UNFOLDS AS CHILDREN MATURE AND ACTIVELY INTERACT WITH THEIR ENVIRONMENT.
>
> - CHILDREN'S LANGUAGE BECOMES MORE COMPLEX OVER TIME AS A RESULT OF NATURAL, CONVERSATIONAL GIVE-AND-TAKE, NOT DIRECT INSTRUCTION AND DRILL.
>
> - CHILDREN LEARN LANGUAGE SKILLS WHEN SIGNIFICANT PEOPLE IN THEIR LIVES LISTEN TO THEM AND RESPOND WITH INTEREST TO THEIR ATTEMPTS TO DESCRIBE THEIR INTENTIONS, THOUGHTS, AND EXPERIENCES.

*Talking about topics that are important to children will encourage them to express their thoughts and feelings.*

---

other adults make. Ask them to be ready to share at the next meeting the impact this had on their conversations.

11. Make a poster titled "Children's Conversational Topics" to display on the parent bulletin board. Add the topics generated by parents in Step #9.

# Child Contributions and Adult Acknowledgments in Conversation

**Child contribution**—an observation or statement your child initiates

**Adult acknowledgment**—a word, phrase, or gesture that you make to let your child know you are listening

1. Brainstorm a list of three or four conversational topics children have talked about with you or other family members or friends. Write these in the space provided. Sample topics:

    MOISTURE ON THE GRASS IN THE MORNING

    TRUCKS PASSING ON THE HIGHWAY AS YOU DRIVE

2. Write down at least three *contributions* your child might make about each topic. Examples:

    "THIS GRASS IS WET."

    "WHEN I GROW UP I WANT TO BE A TRUCK DRIVER, TOO."

3. For each child contribution, write three corresponding *acknowledgments* you could make to keep the lines of communication open and in the hands of your child. Examples:

    "IT SURE IS WET. I WONDER HOW COME?"

    "YOU THINK YOU'D LIKE DRIVING A TRUCK LIKE THAT."

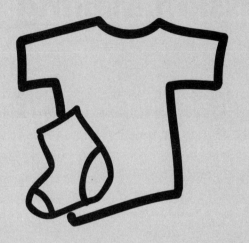

# II.
# Daily
# Routine

# The High/Scope Preschool Daily Routine and How It Encourages Children's Decision Making

## Goals

✔ To share information about how the High/Scope daily routine supports and encourages children to make choices and follow their own interests

✔ To explain the educational benefits children receive when they pursue their own interests

## Materials

- Stick-on name tags
- Magic markers
- Chart 7A (prepared ahead of time on a large piece of chart paper or an overhead transparency)
- Handout titled "Our Daily Routine Schedule and Why We Do It"
- Chart paper and masking tape

## Introduction

1. Welcome parents and explain that you will be discussing how and why the High/Scope daily routine supports and encourages children to pursue their own interests and make choices during the school day.

## Opening Activity

2. Tell parents that you will begin the evening's discussion with a scavenger hunt. Give them 5 minutes to explore their child's classroom and return to the table with an object they find particularly interesting.

3. With the whole group, have parents share the reasons they chose their specific items. Comment on the variety of choices they made, and explain that this freedom to select and use materials is an integral part of the High/Scope Curriculum.

## Central Ideas

4. Display Chart 7A, "Benefits of Pursuing Your Own Interests," and discuss the reasons that choice is crucial to the daily routine and to children's development.

5. Hand out copies of the handout titled "Our Daily Routine Schedule and Why We Do It." Using the handout as a guide, explain your class routine. If desired, attach time frames to each segment of the routine on the handout. Give specific examples of the ways children are encouraged to make decisions and pursue their own interests during each part of the day. For example, share a large-group-time song for which children have added new verses; or display children's small-group-time work, pointing out the different ways children have experimented with similar materials.

> **Chart 7A—Use in Step #4**
> BENEFITS OF PURSUING YOUR OWN INTERESTS
>
> - DEVELOPS DECISION-MAKING SKILLS
> - BUILDS SELF-CONFIDENCE AND DEVELOPS INITIATIVE
> - ENCOURAGES SOCIAL INTERACTION WITH PEERS AND ADULTS
> - HOLDS AND FOCUSES ATTENTION
> - BUILDS ON INDIVIDUAL STRENGTHS
> - CREATES FEELINGS OF SUCCESS AND MASTERY

6. Encourage parents' comments and questions.

## Reflections and Ideas for Applications

7. Give each small group a large piece of chart paper and marker. Ask them to discuss the things that interest their children at home and record them on the paper. For example, one group's chart might list the following: *draws on paper with markers and crayons, races little cars across the living room sofa, puts a blanket over the kitchen table for a tent and reads books underneath.*

8. Hang the charts around the room and point out similar materials that you already have in the classroom or could provide in order to build on children's interests. For example, you might say "We have markers and paper in the art area, and we can add some blankets near the book or block area for children to make tents."

9. Thank parents for their participation. Tell them that a future meeting, "The Importance of Consistent Routines," will address other benefits of providing consistency in a child's daily activities.

10. As parents put back their materials from the opening activity, have them notice how other interests listed on the chart are supported in the classroom.

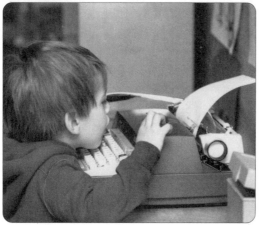

*Activities of their own choosing often capture children's full attention.*

## Follow-up Plans

11. Review the list of children's activities at home. Note any materials, activities, or field trips that might be offered at school to support children's home interests. Announce the classroom additions and upcoming trips on the parent bulletin board.

12. Provide a copy of the video *The High/Scope Curriculum: The Daily Routine* (available from High/Scope Press—see p. 182) for parents to check out from the parent lending library.

# Our Daily Routine Schedule and Why We Do It

## The Schedule

**Plan-work-recall.** Children express their own intentions (plan), follow through on their ideas, interact with people and materials, solve problems as they arise (do), and reflect on and review work-time activities with others (review).

**Snack time.** Children and adults share nutritious foods and meaningful conversations.

**Large-group time.** Children and adults build a sense of community and try out new ideas by participating in singing, movement activities, storytelling, and re-enactments of important events.

**Small-group time.** Adults introduce a common activity with related materials. Children use the materials in ways that are meaningful to them while adults observe, join in, and support children in their discoveries.

**Outside time.** Children engage in vigorous, noisy, physical play as well as quiet reflection. Adults and children both participate in exploring the natural surroundings of an outdoor space, making observations, conversing about those observations, and inventing and playing new games.

## The Rationale for Having a Consistent Daily Routine

A daily routine helps children

- Pursue their own interests
- Have adequate time to persist in their own efforts
- Share control of their learning with others
- Receive support from attentive adults
- Experience flexibility within a predictable sequence of events

# The Importance of Consistent Routines

## Goals

✔ To help parents understand that a consistent routine helps to manage every-day life

✔ To suggest concrete ways to establish consistency in a home routine

## Materials

- Pencils and pens
- Handout titled "Tips for Establishing Supportive Routines"
- An 8½" × 11" piece of paper for each parent

## Introduction

1. Tell parents that you will be focusing tonight on the impact of routines on children and their families.

## Opening Activity

2. Tell parents that this activity will help them see the importance of a pre-dictable routine in one's daily life. Give each person a piece of paper and ask them to tear it into six pieces. When they have finished, have them write down the first six things they do in the morning after they wake up, one activity on each of the six pieces. Then have them lay the strips in order on the table. Ask for volunteers to read their morning routine out loud. When they have done this, have parents randomly shuffle their paper strips, then again have volunteers read the new order out loud.

## Central Ideas

3. Using the exercise they have just completed, help parents see that any change in a routine can create discomfort or even chaos. For example, getting dressed before stepping into the shower doesn't work. Make the point that having con-sistent routines helps free adults from worrying about what they are going to do next and adds security and stability to their day. In pairs or groups of

three, have parents describe a time when their children were upset by a change in routine, such as skipping the bedtime story or having a babysitter instead of Mom pick them up from school. When they have finished, point out that children, like adults, count on the security and stability of a consistent routine.

4. Pass out the handout titled "Tips for Establishing Supportive Routines." As a whole group, review each item on the list and discuss the examples. Allow time for questions and comments.

5. In small groups, have parents share an example of how they have used one of the strategies listed on the "Tips" handout. Meet back as a whole group to share these success stories.

### Reflections and Ideas for Application

6. Ask parents to make a plan for how they might use one or more of the strategies suggested at home.

### Follow-up Plans

7. Ask parents to share their attempts at supporting routines at home, either by writing a note or in a conversation with you. Jot down their success stories on the parent bulletin board.

# Tips for Establishing Supportive Routines

1. **Establish a schedule and be consistent with it.** Be sure that both children and adults can depend on it and follow it without constant reminders. One concrete way to help children follow a routine is to use charts or photos to illustrate the sequence of events in that particular routine. For example, your child's bedtime routine might include bath, teeth brushing, bedtime story, and lights out. To make the sequence of events visual for your child, divide a long strip of paper into four sections. Starting with the left section and progressing to the right, put in each section either a photo of your child doing each of these steps, a stick-figure drawing, or an actual object (like a toothbrush or a book). As your child does each step in the routine, he or she can move a clothespin or a paper clip to the next picture in the sequence.

2. **When there are changes in the routine, describe them in ways that children will understand, using props if necessary.** For example, on the mornings when your child does not go to school, stick a magnet on the refrigerator door with a picture of a house (to symbolize a stay-at-home day) or of the babysitter. On school mornings, use a picture of the school (or school bus if your child rides a bus).

3. **Provide materials for children during their daily routines that will make the experiences active and challenging.** For example, provide bath toys that will stimulate learning, such as sponges, objects that float and sink, and plastic pitchers for pouring and emptying.

4. **As much as possible, allow children to make choices during routines, and then follow their lead.** For example, pretend to sip the cup of "tea" your child pours for you during bath time. Or let your child choose a book for you to read together at bedtime; allow enough time for comments and questions.

5. **Handle challenges to the routine with a calm but firm approach, acknowledging and rephrasing children's messages.** "I don't want to brush my teeth tonight" can be responded to with "You wish you could skip tooth brushing tonight." If that isn't enough, give a reason for the routine: "Brushing our teeth is important because it keeps them healthy." A final strategy includes maintaining the routine firmly while acknowledging the child's emotion: "I'm sorry you're so mad at me, but I really want your teeth to stay clean and healthy."

# Transitions—Smooth Sailing or Daily Struggle?

## Goals

✔ To understand the impact transitions have on adults and children
✔ To offer ideas for making these transitions easier
✔ To apply suggested ideas to real-life situations

## Materials

- Chart pad and markers or overhead projector
- Handouts: "What If It Happened to You?"
    "Daily Transitions"
    "Transition Tips"
    "Which Tip Fits This Scene?"

## Introduction

1. Explain that tonight's discussion will center on the transitions from one activity to another that children experience at home—in particular, how to make them flow more smoothly.

## Opening Activity

2. Pass out the handout "What If It Happened to You?" Ask parents to choose a partner and discuss the ways they might feel and act in the situations presented on the handout.

3. Meet back as a whole group and record some of the parents' reactions on a piece of chart paper. Discuss the ways people respond to a sudden change from one activity or location to another, concentrating on *unwanted* transitions over which they may have little or no control.

## Central Ideas

4. Tell parents that you will look next at some of the transitions their children experience during a typical day at home, as well as the variety of reactions children have to changing from one activity, location, or caregiver to the

next. To help facilitate the discussion, pass out the "Daily Transitions" hand-out. As a large group, discuss the first transition time on the handout. Ask parents for examples of their children's behavior between wake-up time and breakfast, then discuss the possible needs and feelings that might be behind this behavior. Make connections between the feelings children may experience during this transition (confusion, nervousness, anger, resistance, compliance, excitement) and the reactions parents had during the opening activity.

5. Have parents complete the rest of the handout in groups of three or four.

6. Let parents know that although transitions are often difficult for both adults *and* children, consideration of children's feelings will help these changes flow more smoothly. Pass out the handout titled "Transition Tips." As a large group, read through each suggestion and encourage parents to ask questions and make comments.

## Reflections and Ideas for Application

7. Have parents get back into their small groups, and pass out the handout titled "Which Tip Fits This Scene?" Ask groups to match each scenario described to a suggestion from the "Transition Tips" handout.

8. Briefly review the answers to the matching activity with the whole group.

9. Before ending the meeting, ask parents to complete the following sentence with a partner:

   • *One thing I have learned tonight that will help my child with transitions at home is . . .*

## Follow-up Plans

10. Ask parents to write down their transition successes. Post them on the parent news board.

*Remain calm yet firm when children challenge a routine. Acknowledge children's feelings and give them an explanation: "It's hard to stop when you are having fun playing. But now school is over and it's time to go home."*

**HANDOUT**

# What If It Happened to You?

### Scenario One

This is the first sunny Saturday in the 2 weeks since you bought plants for your garden. You are busily (and happily) digging when your spouse yells out the window, "Why are you still digging? We were supposed to be at my mother's house for dinner 20 minutes ago!" You realize you forgot about dinner, and you still have a flat of flowers you want to finish planting.

### Scenario Two

You are a 5-year-old child who has always had a bedroom to yourself. In the last few weeks, in preparation for the new baby and without asking you what *you* like, your parents have been adding furniture and repainting your bedroom walls.

# Daily Transitions

Below are some common transition times in the lives of parents and preschoolers. With your group members, discuss and record some of your own children's behaviors during these times. Next, record what those behaviors may indicate about children's needs and feelings at that moment. If the transition times listed below do not make sense for your family, write your own in the space labeled *Other*.

**From wake-up time to breakfast—**

*Behaviors:*

*Feelings/needs:*

**From the car (or walk, bus, bike) to the classroom—**

*Behaviors:*

*Feelings/needs:*

●●● ▶

**From nighttime playing to bed—**
*Behaviors:*

*Feelings/needs:*

**Other—**
*Behaviors:*

*Feelings/needs:*

●

**HANDOUT**

# Transition Tips

1. **Keep children's routines consistent.** This will free both of you from wondering and worrying about what will come next.

2. **Limit the number of transitions.** The fewer changes children have to make between activities, places, and caregivers, the better.

3. **Plan your transitions so that children can be active, follow their interests, make choices, and have adult support.**

4. **Consider children's developmental abilities and maintain realistic expectations.** When possible, use visual clues to help children better understand transitions.

5. **When children balk at a routine, try to remain flexible and calm.** Resist the temptation to scold and shame children.

6. **Pay attention to behaviors that signal children need a change in routine.** You can often do so without compromising your goal.

**HANDOUT**

# Which Tip Fits This Scene?

Read the scenarios listed below. Decide as a group which strategy from the "Transition Tips" handout best describes each scenario, and write the number (or numbers) of the strategy in the space provided below. When the scenarios described could be improved upon based on the strategy your group has selected, discuss why and how the improvement could be made.

A. _____ You are waiting in an extremely long line at the grocery store. You want to pass the time by browsing through a magazine from the display, but you notice that your daughter is beginning to get restless and hungry. You tell her she can pick pretzels or crackers to munch on while you wait.

B. _____ You have a bedtime routine where your daughter takes a bath, has a snack, brushes her teeth, and then picks out a book you read together. While she is brushing her teeth one night, you run to answer the phone. When you come back 2 minutes later, she has pulled most of the dental floss out of the container, and it is lying in a tangled pile on the floor.

C. _____ Every day when your son comes home from school, you have a routine. First you read a book, then he plays while you cook dinner, then you eat together and play some more, and then he starts to get ready for bed.

D. _____ Usually you read a story to both of your children before bedtime. Lately, your younger child has been disrupting the story, preferring to play with the train set in the room next to his bedroom. He willingly comes to bed after you finish reading to your older child.

E. _____ Your youngest child just started school. Each morning when she wakes up the first thing she says is, "Is this a school day?" You decide to take a picture of her school and a picture of your apartment. Each night, you place near her bed the picture of the place where she will spend the following day.

F. _____ You have signed up your son for soccer, piano lessons, and a neighborhood play group. Soccer meets twice a week and the others meet once. You notice your son says he's tired a lot and complains about a stomachache, but the doctor says there is nothing physically wrong with him.

# Cleaning, Shopping, Laundry, Home Repairs, Cooking, AND Playing With My Child?!

## Goals

✔ To look at ways parents can spend meaningful time with their children while doing household chores

✔ To help parents discover what children learn when they help parents with chores

## Materials

- Chart pad and markers

- Handouts: "Supporting Children's Interest in Helping Out at Home"
  "An Action Plan for Chores"
  "High/Scope Preschool Key Experiences" (see pp. 36–37)

- Prop boxes: Gather real materials that are suitable for children to use while parents are doing specific jobs around the house. Cleaning supplies might include a squirt bottle filled with water, a dust rag, a hand vacuum, and a dust pan and whisk broom. A cooking box might include wire whisks, potato mashers, measuring spoons, plastic bowls, ravioli rollers, pastry brushes, and pie plates, as well as items (such as play dough) that children could use along with these tools to imitate adults' actions.

## Introduction

1. Ask how many parents had other responsibilities at home that might have kept them from coming to the meeting. (If there are any who do not raise their hands, ask them what their secret is for getting everything done!) Acknowledge that parents do have many responsibilities around the house in addition to raising their children. Tell parents that you hope tonight's discussion will give them some practical ways to spend meaningful time with their children while taking care of their household duties.

## Opening Activity

2. Give each group of three to four parents a piece of chart paper and markers. Ask parents to list the responsibilities they have in maintaining their home

(excluding their job outside the home and duties directly involving children, such as bathing, chauffeuring, caring for them when sick). After about 5 minutes, ask them to post the lists around the room.

### Central Ideas

3.  As a whole group, look at the charts. Expect the responsibilities listed to include things like *gardening, washing dishes, cooking dinner, shopping for groceries, doing laundry, cleaning the house, making repairs.* Acknowledge that all these demands on parents' time can make them wonder how they can find time to interact with their children. Tell them that you would like to share some ideas for balancing these demands by including children in their household duties.

4.  Pass out the handout "Supporting Children's Interest in Helping Out at Home." Have parents divide into five small groups. Assign each group *one* of the strategies on the handout to read and discuss. Ask each group to then explain their item to the whole group and discuss some of the benefits of the strategy for both children and adults.

5.  Explain to parents that the next exercise will help them choose some specific ways to actively include their children in household chores. Pass out the handout "An Action Plan for Chores," and ask parents to meet in groups of three to four to complete the exercise.

*Parents can provide space and materials for children to play alongside them as they take care of household tasks.*

6. Ask parents to share with the whole group additional ideas they have thought of.

## Reflections and Ideas for Application

7. Pass out the key experience handout. Show parents a few items from one of the prop boxes and ask them for ideas on how their children might use them while parents are doing similar chores around the house. Then have them look for key experiences that would be supported by those activities.

8. Have parents continue Step #7 in small groups, each group using its own prop box.

9. Ask parents to share their ideas with the whole group.

## Follow-up Plans

10. Make prop boxes available as part of the lending library so that parents can check them out and experiment with using the materials at home. Ask for parents' feedback and additional suggestions for the boxes.

11. On the parent bulletin board, display the ideas generated by parents on the "Action Plan for Chores" handout. Encourage parents to add to the list based on their observations from home.

**HANDOUT**

# Supporting Children's Interest in Helping Out at Home

1. **Take cues from your child.** Children differ in what they like to do while you are working around the house. Some like to be involved in the chores while others may prefer private play time. If you have just gotten home from work, your child may want your undivided attention for a few minutes before you begin the meal or start laundry. Pay close attention to what he or she says and does during these times. Use those messages to establish a routine that will work for both of you.

2. **When finding ways to include children in the job at hand, plan around their strengths and interests.** Young children enjoy imitating the actions of others, so they are often interested in participating in household chores. Like grownups, they, too, prefer some activities over others. Some children like to take the sheets off the bed and throw them in the washing machine; other children like to dig in the dirt and help plant and weed the garden. Figure out which chores your child likes to do, and plan to support those interests in active ways as you complete your routine jobs around the house.

3. **Expect that your child's help and participation may result in extra work for you.** Remember, you have had a lot of practice cleaning, cooking, washing, and doing other household chores. Children will need similar practice to achieve the level of skill you have. Balance the short-term inconvenience of their "help" with the knowledge that in the long run, their feelings of success and interaction with you are more important.

4. **When including your child in your routine tasks, remember the ingredients of active learning: materials, manipulation, choice, language from the child, and adult support.** Use these to help you judge whether the materials you provide and the conversations you have while working together are meaningful to your child. For example, you could give your daughter a bowl of water, a wire whisk, and a chair to reach the countertop so she can work alongside while you prepare a casserole for the evening's meal.

5. **As much as possible, keep a consistent routine when doing chores.** Children rely on consistency to understand and predict what will come next. Some families, for example, make a trip to the Laundromat on a certain day of the week or water the houseplants in a certain order.

# An Action Plan for Chores

Listed below are some common household chores. Think about your own child's abilities and interests and circle the tasks below that you think your child might be able to participate in with you. Create a new category if the ideas listed do not have meaning for your household, or if you want to add ideas from your own experience that are not on the list. Discuss with your group members.

### Gardening

Shovel dirt into a wheelbarrow
Stick bulbs into the earth
Water plants with a hose or
    sprinkling can
Pick ripe tomatoes from the vine
Pull out weeds
Other:

### Grocery shopping

Put can and bottle returns in
    machines
Hold the list and help look for specific
    items
Get items from the shelf to put in cart
Push the cart down aisle
Take groceries out to put on scanner
Other:

### Cooking

Wipe the counter
Crack an egg into a bowl
Pour batter into muffin tins
Tear lettuce leaves for a salad
Set the table
Other:

### Laundry

Collect dirty towels and bedding
Empty the clothes from hamper into
    laundry basket
Put clothes and detergent into washer
Throw clothes into dryer
Insert money into machines
Other:

# 11 Don't Be Surprised if Your Child Wants to Plan at Home on Saturdays

## Goals

✔ To help parents understand that children want to and are able to express their own intentions and ideas for doing something

✔ To suggest how parents can encourage and support children's intentions at home

## Materials

- Chart 11A (prepared ahead of time on a large sheet of chart paper or an overhead transparency)
- Chart pad and markers or overhead projector
- Handouts: "Saying 'Yes' to Children's Desire to Plan"
  "My Child's Planning Habits"

## Introduction

1. Tell parents that tonight you will talk about children's expression of their own ideas and intentions—called *planning*—and why it is important. Tell them you will also discuss ways they can encourage and support this growing ability and confidence children have to express and put into action their ideas and intentions.

## Opening Activity

2. Ask parents to imagine that they have a free day to do whatever they wish. Tell them to talk with two or three others about what they would do with this 12-hour gift of time. Ask them to list the things they would need to prepare in order to successfully carry out their ideas.

## Central Ideas

3. After a few minutes, bring the whole group back together. Display Chart 11A, "Why Planning Is Important," and discuss the points listed on the chart in connection with the activity in Step #2.

4. Next, have parents imagine that it is the morning of the day to do what they have planned, and just as they are about to get started, their work supervisor calls with a list of ten things that HAVE to be done TODAY. Record parents' reactions to this scenario on chart paper. They might make such comments as "It wouldn't be as enjoyable." "I would be mad." "I would do it because I had to." "All my plans would be for nothing." "I might never get another chance to do what I'd wanted to do."

**Chart 11A—Use in Step #3**
WHY PLANNING IS IMPORTANT

- HELPS TO VIEW ONESELF AS A "CAN-DO, MAKE-THINGS-HAPPEN" PERSON

- PROMOTES SELF-CONFIDENCE AND A SENSE OF CONTROL

- LEADS TO A DEEPER INVOLVEMENT WITH AND CONCENTRATION ON WORK OR PLAY

- ALLOWS INDIVIDUALS TO TAKE ON CHALLENGES APPROPRIATE TO THEIR OWN INTERESTS AND ABILITIES

- HELPS PEOPLE LEARN TO PLAN MORE COMPLEX PROJECTS

5. Have parents divide into groups of three or four. Give each group a piece of chart paper and a marker. Ask them to discuss and write down some of the ideas that their children express in the car on the way to school, or plans they suggest for the weekend or evenings.

## Reflections and Ideas for Application

6. Post the lists around the room and point out that it is not uncommon (as they can see by the lists) for young children to have lots of ideas of what they want to do, nor is it uncommon for adults to feel uncomfortable when children "take charge" in this way. Parents may even fear that they are losing control of situations at home as, for example, their daughter announces that her plan is to finish looking at a book *before* the family goes grocery shopping.

7. Tell parents that you would like to encourage them to support their children's intentions by introducing some strategies for them to try at home. Pass out the handout titled "Saying 'Yes' to Children's Desire to Plan." Ask parents to return to their small groups and follow the directions on the handout.

8. Meet back as a whole group to review each small group's conclusions.

## Follow-up Plans

9. Pass out the handout titled "My Child's Planning Habits." Ask parents to take it home and for the next 2 weeks jot down notes on the handout as they notice their own children planning at home. After 2 weeks, display their observations on the parent bulletin board.

# Saying "Yes" to Children's Desire to Plan

Read the list of support strategies below. Identify one or more that you could use to support your child in each of the scenarios that follow. Record your group's reactions in the space provided, rewriting the scenario when necessary.

## Support Strategies for Encouraging Children's Intentions and Ideas

1. Relax and enjoy the opportunity to discover your child's thoughts and ideas about things.
2. Set aside a time for your child to plan when you are not distracted by chores or other household duties.
3. Ask for your child's plans and listen attentively. Pay attention not only to your child's words but also to gestures and other nonverbal messages.
4. As your child's plans become more detailed, provide materials, conversations, and experiences to support your child's efforts.
5. Keep from inadvertently imposing your own ideas on your child—for example, by saying "Oh, you did that yesterday—wouldn't you rather _____ ?" or "You never ask your sister to join you, and she really wants to. Maybe you could play with her today."

## Scenarios

A. _____ It is Saturday morning. Your child wakes you up at 7:00 and announces, "Today I want you to read me this story, then give me some crayons and paper so I can draw my favorite part of the story."

●●●▶

B. \_\_\_\_ You decide to try out the following planning idea at home: your son will have time to decide activities 30 minutes before dinner each night and on Saturday mornings before you grocery shop and do laundry. You are ready to give up after 2 weeks because every time you ask him what he wants to do, he says something vague like "Build something," or he starts barking like a dog and running all over the house.

C. \_\_\_\_ Your daughter loves to paint and draw and almost always chooses this as her plan at home. You would like to support her ideas, but you also think it's getting too expensive to buy all the supplies she uses.

# My Child's Planning Habits

Ideas my child has had:

Ways he or she expresses these ideas (gestures, actions, words):

Activities and ideas he or she often repeats:

Variations he or she has made to plans over time:

# Reading at Home

## Goals

✔ To practice critiquing selected children's books
✔ To share ways parents can involve children in reading storybooks and other print material
✔ To help parents understand why reading at home is so important

## Materials

- An assortment of current and classic children's storybooks
- Handouts: "Book Selection Guidelines"
  "Tips for Reading at Home"
- Chart 12A (prepared ahead of time on a large piece of chart paper or an overhead transparency)

## Introduction

1. Tell parents you will be discussing children's storybooks, the value in providing a variety of reading materials for young children, and ways parents can make reading an interactive, educational experience.

## Opening Activity

2. In small groups of two or three, have parents discuss their own reading preferences, focusing on *what* they like to read and the *setting* that makes reading the most pleasurable for them.

3. As a large group, ask parents to share some of their responses. Emphasize that there is a wide range of reading materials available to people and that they read what is most interesting to them (*Car and Driver* or *Family Fun* magazines, a daily newspaper, the advertised specials at their favorite grocery store, mystery novels, historical books). Highlight also some of the pleasurable reading spots indicated by parents (on a soft sofa, in bed before going to sleep, outdoors in the warm sun).

4. Point out that like adults, children also need a variety of reading materials in their environment and comfortable places to look at those materials.

*Encourage parents to read a variety of books and other print materials with children as often as possible.*

### Central Ideas

5. Ask parents to share how they choose books for their children—for instance, they might pick those they liked as children themselves, or subjects their children are interested in, or books with colorful pictures. Pass out the "Book Selection Guidelines" handout and two or three storybooks to each group of four or five parents. Ask for volunteers in each group to take turns reading the books out loud to their group members, then have the groups evaluate the books using the checklist on the handout.

6. To the whole group, explain that selecting quality reading materials is only one part of introducing children to the world of reading. Reading to and with children regularly creates a close physical and emotional bond; children begin to associate the satisfaction of warm human relationships with stories and reading. Sharing books at home also helps emphasize the importance of reading.

7. Pass out the handout titled "Tips for Reading at Home." Go over the points together and encourage comments and questions.

## Reflections and Ideas for Application

8. Ask parents to pair up with their spouse, significant other, or one other person. Ask each pair to answer the questions written on Chart 12A.

## Follow-up Plans

9. Encourage parents to check books out of your program's parent lending library. If you do not already have one, start a collection of donated books, books from garage sales and library sales, etc. Two additional resources are the *High/Scope Preschool Classroom Library* and the *Grandpa's Choice* Series, both available from High/Scope Press (see p. 181).

10. Plan a field trip to the local library and invite parents to come along. Ask the librarian to recommend 20 popular storybooks for preschool-aged children. Photocopy the list; put one copy on the parent news board, and make additional copies available for parents to take home for their own reference.

**Chart 12A—Use in Step #8**

• THE BEST TIME OF DAY FOR ME TO READ ON A REGULAR BASIS WITH MY CHILD IS . . .

• ONE WAY I WILL INVOLVE MY CHILD IN READING IS . . .

• THREE NEW PLACES I WILL STORE BOOKS IN MY HOME ARE . . .

• TWO TYPES OF READING MATERIALS (OTHER THAN STORYBOOKS) THAT I WILL READ WITH MY CHILD ARE . . .

**HANDOUT**

# Book Selection Guidelines

Evaluate your group's storybooks using the following criteria.

1. **Illustrations.** Are the drawings, paintings, or photographs visually pleasing? If there are people shown in the pictures, do they represent a variety of races, ages, and physical abilities? What are the people doing? Are the activities and messages depicted meaningful to your children and ones that you want them to see?

   *Title of book:*

   *Comments:*

   *Title of book:*

   *Comments:*

●●● ▶

2. **Story line.** Will it make sense to children? Is it interesting enough to encourage children to discuss it? Is it written in the language your child speaks?

   *Title of book:*

   *Comments:*

   *Title of book:*

   *Comments:*

3. **Child interest.** Will the subject of the book be of interest to your child? Will it make your child laugh, cry, or feel curious about something? Is it a book your child will look at alone, when no adult is available for reading?

   *Title of book:*

   *Comments:*

   *Title of book:*

   *Comments:*

●●● ▶

**4. Adult interest.** Is this a book that interests *you?* Is it a book you want to sit down with your child and talk about?

*Title of book:*

*Comments:*

*Title of book:*

*Comments:*

**HANDOUT**

# Tips for Reading at Home

1. **Try to read a book with your child at least once a day.** Having a specific time (for example, after school or before bed) and a comfortable location for reading will help your child anticipate and look forward to the ritual. Let your child select the book, and don't be surprised if he or she picks the same book several days in a row. When you read with your child, encourage a conversation about the storyline, the pictures, and the characters.

2. **Store books in various places throughout your house or apartment so that your child can have easy access to them.** For instance, put them in a low kitchen cupboard, in a basket in the bathroom, in a crate in the bedroom, and on a bookshelf in the living room.

3. **Join your local public library and take your child along when you go to select books.** Remember to check out books for yourself, too, so your child sees that reading is important to *you*.

4. **On walks with your child around your community, read road signs, license plates, street signs, house numbers, and makes of cars.**

5. **Encourage your child to look at family photos.** Make a game of telling stories about the people and places in the photos. This is an early part of the reading process and will encourage your child to help "read" a storybook by looking at the pictures.

6. **Let your child look at your grocery list.** Encourage him or her to create a grocery list using pictures of the products, especially items your child uses.

7. **Read cereal boxes, letters from friends, or interesting newspaper articles out loud to your child.**

# III.
# Learning
# Environment

# 13 Too Many Toys, Too Many Small Parts? Looking for Order in the Mess!

## Goals

✔ To look at how important physical space is to completing work and play tasks
✔ To offer practical strategies for reducing toy clutter and displaying children's creations at home

## Materials

- Chart 13A (prepared ahead of time on a large sheet of chart paper or an overhead transparency)

- A variety of storage containers in different shapes and sizes, such as sturdy cardboard boxes, plastic crates and dishpans, simple wooden shelves, hanging pegboards, baskets, plastic wastepaper cans, plastic silverware trays, and hanging three-tiered metal baskets

- Several photocopies* of "The Effects of Arranging and Equipping Space According to High/Scope Guidelines" (Mary Hohmann and David P. Weikart, *Educating Young Children: Active Learning Practices for Preschool and Child Care Programs,* 1995, pp. 123–124)

*Parents—like teachers!—often feel overwhelmed by children's toy clutter.*

## Introduction

1. Ask parents if they have ever felt like their house has been taken over by toys. Tell them that tonight you will be discussing the way children's

---

*Please see p. 12 for information on copying High/Scope publications.

play spaces at home influence their ability to take initiative and follow through on their own ideas. Tell them you will also be looking at how children's favorite toys and materials might be stored to minimize clutter and help children keep track of their things.

*Have parents tour the classroom to get some ideas for storage items they can use at home, such as plastic crates and containers, shoeboxes, dishpans, baskets, silverware trays, and plastic jars.*

## Opening Activity

2. Ask parents to think about a specific space in their home, garage, yard, or workplace where they feel relaxed and able to work or play effectively. Have them describe this place to another person and tell their partner what makes it so comfortable for them.

3. Ask parents to share some of the reasons their spaces are conducive to work or play, and list these on a large piece of chart paper. Here are some examples they might share: "It has enough space." "All my tools are nearby." "The chairs are comfortable." "I can be alone." "I can talk to others."

## Central Ideas

4. Review with the group the points on Chart 13A (on the following page). Ask parents to return to their partners and describe to them some of the ways their own children use spaces at home to explore, pretend, and make up games.

5. As a whole group, discuss the similarities between the way adults arrange their own environments to promote work output and how parents can structure children's environments in order for children to accomplish *their* goals. Expect responses such as "Provide a table surface." "Store toys where he can reach them without asking me." "Find a container big enough to hold all her Barbie doll stuff."

**Chart 13A—Use in Step #4**
YOUNG CHILDREN NEED SPACES WHERE THEY CAN . . .

- EXPLORE, BUILD, PRETEND, AND DRAW—ALONE AND WITH OTHERS
- FIND, USE, AND RETURN MATERIALS THEY NEED AS THEY MAKE UP THEIR OWN GAMES AND ACTIVITIES
- FEEL SAFE, VALUED, ADVENTUROUS, AND COMPETENT

6. Give the group a few minutes to tour the classroom. Ask them to search for one item that they know would be of interest to their own child, one storage container, and something that could make children feel safe and valued.

7. Have parents divide up into groups of four each. Give them time to share the items they found and to brainstorm ways they could use these or similar items at home.

## Reflections and Ideas for Application

8. Give parents a few minutes to look at the various storage containers you brought. Ask them to think about their child's most difficult toy to store—something very large, perhaps, or a set with several small pieces. Ask parents to draw on some of the ideas presented tonight and jot down a way they could store this toy when they get home.

## Follow-up Plans

9. Give parents a copy of the *Educating Young Children* article (see *Materials*) to take home and read. Put a dry erase board near the parent area in the classroom for them to jot down notes about how organizing their child's space at home helped the child take initiative or solve a problem.

# 14 Finding Noncommercial Active Learning Materials

## Goals

✔ To examine noncommercial objects and materials that interest children

✔ To look at the variety of ways children might use these materials and the kinds of things children learn as they play with them

## Materials

- A variety of natural, scrap, and authentic materials, such as sticks, stones, seashells, pine cones, empty food containers, toilet paper rolls, margarine tub lids, cardboard boxes, old steering wheels, envelopes and stamps, empty shampoo bottles, wood scraps, empty seed packets, flowerpots, whiskbrooms and dustpans, old wallets and purses, suitcases, cameras, and kitchen utensils; also dress-up clothing like neckties, jewelry, jackets, and hats

- Chart pad and markers

- Masking tape

- Chart 14A (prepared ahead of time on a large sheet of chart paper or an overhead transparency)

- Key experience handout for each small group (see pp. 36–37)

## Introduction

1. Tell parents that tonight you will be looking at free or low-cost materials children can play with that can be found around the house or in natural settings, or obtained from local businesses. Explain that together you will identify ways children might play with these materials and discuss what they can learn from their experiences with them.

## Opening Activity

2. Have parents break into groups of five to six each. Give each group a marker, a piece of chart paper, and a bag containing three or four items listed under *Materials*. Ask parents to write down the different ways they imagine their child might use each of the items in their bag. For example, a child might

scrape the pine cone with his fingernails to feel the roughness or to listen to the sound it makes.

3. After 10 minutes, ask groups to display their papers on a table or wall. Give everyone 5 minutes to walk around and read what the other groups have written. Walk around with them and highlight ideas that fit into the categories on Chart 14A. Be sure you mark at least one suggestion from each group.

> **Chart 14A—Use in Step #4**
> WHAT KINDS OF MATERIALS CAN CHILDREN EXPLORE FROM...
>
> • HOME (THINGS THEY SEE ADULTS USING):
>
> • NATURE:
>
> • THE COMMUNITY:

### Central Ideas

4. Gather back as a whole group. Using the groups' charts for reference, comment on the variety of experiences children enjoy when they are free to explore materials in their own way. Point out the ideas you highlighted on the groups' charts and connect each to one of the categories on Chart 14A. Ask parents for additional examples of materials children use to learn about home, nature, and their surrounding community.

5. Have parents break into small groups again, and give each group a copy of the key experience handout. Ask groups to find some key experiences that children engage in when they use the materials listed on their original chart.

6. Have each group share one or two of their key experiences with the whole group. Reinforce the notion that when adults provide appropriate everyday materials for children to use in open-ended ways, children's emerging abilities are supported and adults can enjoy watching children's development.

### Reflections and Ideas for Application

7. Ask the small groups to generate a list of places in the community that might be willing to donate surplus materials to the classroom and individual families. Help parents get started by asking them about ways their own businesses might contribute. For example, a hair salon might donate old hand-held hair dryers (with the cords cut off); a fast-food establishment might donate take-out boxes, paper napkins, or menus; or a business office might give away some surplus paper.

8. Share the lists with the whole group. Ask for volunteers to solicit donations of materials, pick them up, and bring them to the center.

### Follow-up Plans

9. Make a spot in your classroom for parents to drop off donations of natural, scrap, and authentic materials. Add some to your classroom and make the rest available for parents to take home and use.

10. Take pictures of children using the everyday materials during work time, and plan some small-group times where children use these materials. On the parent bulletin board, display the pictures or children's creations along with a note identifying appropriate key experience areas.

# 15 Using Classroom Interest Areas as Keys to Gift Buying

## Goals

✔ To use children's choices in the classroom interest areas as a guideline for determining appropriate gift ideas

✔ To generate a list of nontraditional gift ideas and places in the community where they might be purchased

## Materials

- Chart pad and markers

- Photos or slides of children working in the different interest areas of your classroom. If photos from your own classroom are unavailable, photocopy* a collection of pictures from *Educating Young Children* (Mary Hohmann and David P. Weikart, 1995) that show children involved in a variety of actions and experiences. Be sure to include pictures of children *creating with art materials* (play dough, "slime," paint, markers); *using real tools and equipment* (pots and pans in the house area, hammers and screwdrivers in the construction area); *building and pretending* (creating block structures; dressing up in hats, shoes, and jewelry); and *engaged in physical activity* (throwing balls at targets, jumping, and climbing).

- Five wrapped boxes
    *Box 1:* Real tools (hand mixer, pots and pans, hammer, Styrofoam)
    *Box 2:* Household items (wire whisk, egg separator, pancake turner)
    *Box 3:* Art supplies (play dough, markers, paper, tape)
    *Box 4:* Movement supplies (sneakers, balls, targets, streamers)
    *Box 5:* Pretending supplies (suitcase filled with dress-up clothing)

- Handout titled "Where to Shop and What to Buy to Support Children's Interests"

## Introduction

1. Ask parents if they have ever wanted to mute television advertising that features the latest fad toy, or wished for a department store where they did

---

*Please see p. 12 for information on copying High/Scope publications.

not have to walk through the toy section to get to everything else. Tell
parents you will be looking at how to choose gift toys that are not elaborate
or expensive but that support and extend their children's interests at school
and at home.

### Opening Activity

2. Ask parents to meet in groups of three or four each. Give each group a piece
   of chart paper, markers, and several pictures of children working in the classroom. Ask them to write down words and phrases that describe the actions
   and interests of the children in the photos, such as *hauling, digging, pretending, reading,* and *pouring.*

### Central Ideas

3. As a whole group, review the list of action words. Point out that the things
   children are doing in the photos reflect their own interests. Selecting one
   action word as an example, together make a list of materials adults could
   provide to support or expand on this interest. For example, if the child in a
   photo is pouring, the list might include materials such as turkey basters;
   water wheels; various sizes of plastic pitchers, containers, and bottles; sand,
   water, and cooking oil; a bathtub, sink, and kiddie pool.

4. Divide into small groups and ask parents to select two additional words from
   their list and repeat the process outlined in Step #3. When they have finished, post their lists and look at them with the whole group. Be sure to
   emphasize the point that many of the items are commonly found at home
   rather than in a toy store.

5. To tie together children's interests and everyday materials, make the following points:

   • Children enjoy building, pretending, climbing, jumping, getting messy,
     and creating.

   • Children decide how to use materials based on their own intentions and
     ideas.

   • Because of their individuality, children will choose a variety of materials
     to accomplish similar goals.

   • To support children's interests, provide a variety of everyday materials for
     them to explore.

### Reflections and Ideas for Application

6. Pass out one wrapped box to each small group. Ask them to open it and talk
   about where the items inside might have been purchased and how their own
   children might use them while playing at home. Ask parents to share some
   of their ideas with the whole group. Discuss places where they might buy
   gifts that would support their children's interest in these activities, such as

*Displaying photos of the children using various classroom materials can give parents ideas for gift buying. The children pictured here are (a) creating with play dough (b) drawing, and (c) styling a doll's hair.*

garage sales, second-hand shops, hardware departments, art-supply stores, and kitchen-supply shops.

7. Ask parents to meet with a partner to fill out the handout titled "Where to Shop and What to Buy to Support Children's Interests." After they have had a chance to go through the exercise, ask for a few volunteers to share some of their ideas.

### Follow-up Plans

8. Encourage parents to snap pictures of their children playing with the type of gifts suggested at the meeting. Display the photos on a classroom bulletin board along with parent anecdotes. Make a camera available to families without access to one.

**HANDOUT**

# Where to Shop and What to Buy to Support Children's Interests

Share with your partner a few things that interest your child at home. Then make a list of materials that would support and enhance this play. Remember to include materials already found in your home, like sinks, spray bottles, cardboard boxes, backyard swings, etc. Finally, write down your final idea for a gift to buy and the place you would most likely obtain it.

*Child's interests:*

*Materials to support these interests:*

*Gift idea and place of purchase:*

# The Value of Outdoor Play

## Goal

✔ To examine the value of outdoor play and the specific learning opportunities it presents to children

## Materials

- Chart pad and markers or overhead projector
- Charts 16A and 16B (prepared ahead of time on a large piece of chart paper or an overhead transparency)
- Handouts: "What Children Are Doing When They Play Outdoors"
           "High/Scope Preschool Key Experiences" (see pp. 36–37)

## Introduction

1. Tell parents that you will be looking tonight at the value of outdoor play for their children and some specific learning opportunities it presents.

## Opening Activity

2. Ask parents to choose a partner or two and answer the questions listed on Chart 16A.

3. With the whole group, record on the chart some of the group's responses. Responses might include the following: activities—*running, digging, splashing, jumping, climbing, yelling;* materials—*dirt, puddles, hoses, swings, bugs, trees;* and differences—*freer, messier, different smells and sounds.*

> ### Chart 16A—Use in Step #2
> - DESCRIBE SOME OF YOUR FAVORITE OUTDOOR ACTIVITIES FROM CHILDHOOD.
> - WHAT KINDS OF OUTDOOR MATERIALS (NATURAL, COMMERCIAL, HOMEMADE) DID YOU LIKE TO USE AS A CHILD?
> - HOW WAS YOUR OUTDOOR PLAY DIFFERENT FROM YOUR INDOOR PLAY?
>
> ACTIVITIES          MATERIALS          DIFFERENCES

## Central Ideas

4. Ask parents what they feel they learned or gained from these early outdoor experiences. List their answers on chart paper. They may include *got better at sports, learned about spiders and bugs, learned how to cooperate in a game.* Also ask parents how these early outdoor experiences may have prepared them for adulthood. For instance, physical strength is important for carrying a sleeping 4-year-old from the car into the house or for rearranging office or household furniture.

5. Share with parents the benefits of outdoor play as listed on Chart 16B. Where possible, tie in their own answers from Step #4. Give parents a few minutes to make comments, ask questions, or add to the list.

> ### Chart 16B—Use in Step #5
> OUTDOOR PLAY OFFERS . . .
>
> - AN OPPORTUNITY TO EXERCISE VIGOROUSLY AND DEVELOP LARGE-MUSCLE AND COORDINATION SKILLS
> - A CHANCE TO EXPERIENCE FRESH AIR, SUN, CLOUDS, RAIN, WIND, AND SNOW
> - A VEHICLE FOR EXPLORING BUGS, ANTS, SPIDERS, SQUIRRELS, AND NATURAL OBJECTS LIKE STICKS, STONES, LEAVES, ACORNS, AND CHESTNUTS
> - AN OPPORTUNITY TO INTERACT SIDE BY SIDE OR IN COOPERATION WITH OTHER CHILDREN
> - AN OCCASION FOR ADULTS TO OBSERVE CHILDREN IN A FREER ENVIRONMENT AND TO PLAY WITH THEM IN WAYS THAT ARE NOT ALWAYS POSSIBLE INDOORS

## Reflections and Ideas for Application

6. Pass out the handouts "What Children Are Doing When They Play Outdoors" and "High/Scope Preschool Key Experiences." Ask parents to meet together in groups of three to four and follow the directions on the first handout.

7. Meet again as a whole group and write down some of the results of the group discussions. As you do so, you might want to rephrase in more general terms the key experiences that parents list. For example, if parents say, "Children are collaborating," you might write *collaborating* and say, "Yes, children are learning to get along with others." Or, you might mention that *moving in locomotor ways* means children are using different body movements.

## Follow-up Plans

8. Ask parents to make a commitment to play with their child outside, either at the school or at a neighborhood park, before the next scheduled parent meeting.

*Outdoor play is not just for children! Joining in children's outdoor play gives adults a great opportunity to find out more about children's interests and discoveries.*

Ideas for interaction include swinging on a swing, riding on a spring-based teeter-totter, digging in a sand pile, making footprints in the snow, writing with chalk on the sidewalk, or throwing a ball back and forth against a wall or to each other.

9. Place a poster near the bulletin board titled "We Did _____ Outside." Encourage parents to fill in their outdoor adventure stories.

**HANDOUT**

# What Children Are Doing When They Play Outdoors

Read the following scenarios and decide which key experiences from the key experience handout apply to each situation. Record these in the space provided.

## Scenario One

Three-year-old Justin is sitting inside a small sandbox by himself. He has a small dump truck and a spoon. For 15 minutes, he spoons dirt into the back of the dump truck and moves the truck along the edge of the sandbox, turning his body around in a circle. When he gets back to where he started, he dumps out the sand and begins the process all over again. As he works, he says "Vroom" and makes other truck noises.

*Key experiences:*

## Scenario Two

A group of neighborhood children, aged 4, 5, and 7, are playing a game that looks similar to hopscotch. They have drawn various shapes on the ground and are taking turns throwing a stone into one of the shapes. When a stone lands inside a shape, the child who threw it shouts out a movement (run, walk, crawl, hop, twirl) for everyone to do until the child yells "Stop!" Then they all land on the ground, giggling and laughing, and the next person takes a turn. Occasionally they stop and debate the rules—"You have to jump until I say stop"—or make a comment—"My legs are getting tired."

*Key experiences:*

## Scenario Three

At a neighborhood park with your child, you sit on the bench watching children play. You see two children swinging and three children climbing up the ladder and going down the slide. You also see a cluster of children in the sand area. They have collected acorns, chestnuts, and sticks of various sizes and have arranged them in separate piles. They are playing a game using the acorns as money and the sticks to stir the chestnuts to make "soup." Children wanting a bowl of soup give money to the "cook."

*Key experiences:*

# Bringing Outdoor Play Indoors—Creating an Atmosphere for Exuberant Play

## Goals

✔ To look at the benefits of a physically stimulating indoor environment
✔ To list ways children can be physically active inside, even in small spaces

## Materials

- Open area of meeting room where parents can freely throw and catch objects
- An assortment of soft throwing objects, such as wadded-up newspaper, rolled-up socks, and Koosh balls
- Bell
- Charts 17A and 17B (prepared ahead of time on a large sheet of chart paper or an overhead transparency)
- Handout titled "I Think I Can Live With . . ."
- Chart pad and markers or overhead projector

## Introduction

1. Ask parents if they have ever sent their children outside because they have been too boisterous for indoor play, or whether they dread bad-weather days when children cannot go outside. Reassure them that children's natural loud and active behavior does not have to be restricted to the outdoors. Tell parents that tonight you will be looking at the benefits of creating a physically stimulating *indoor* environment for children, as well as ways to support children in their need to be loud and active.

## Opening Activity

2. Give each parent an object to throw. Ask them to spread out around the room and find a spot where they can see everyone in the group. Encourage them to assume different positions (crouching, standing, kneeling, sitting on the floor).

3. When they are positioned, ask them either to make eye contact with one other parent in the room and begin a game of catch and toss or to toss their

object up in the air and catch it themselves. After 2 minutes, ring a bell and tell everyone to move to a new spot, then begin throwing again. Repeat this several times. Expect that the noise level of the room will increase during this activity.

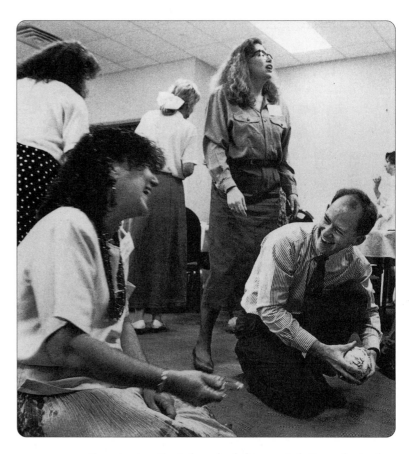

*Engaging in active indoor play helps parents better understand the benefits it offers their children.*

### Central Ideas

4. Gather back as a whole group, and ask parents what stands out in their minds about this activity. Expect parents to make statements like these: "It felt good to do something different." "It felt strange to be playing." "I liked doing something I can do well." "I didn't even notice the noise." "It felt good to laugh and move around after sitting at my job all day." "It was fun and relaxing." If parents voice concerns about the noise level or chaotic nature of the activity, acknowledge the concern and label the feeling: "This kind of play can get loud and boisterous, and we will certainly look at parents' comfort levels later."

5. Show parents Chart 17A, "Benefits of Exuberant Indoor Play." Ask them to comment, question, or add to the list.

6. Pass out the handout titled "I Think I Can Live With . . . " to parents. Ask them to meet in groups of two or three and complete the handout following the instructions.

7. As a whole group, ask parents from each group to list one of the benefits they discussed. Write their comments on chart paper or an overhead transparency.

**Chart 17A—Use in Step #5**
BENEFITS OF EXUBERANT INDOOR PLAY

- RELEASE OF TENSION
- FREEDOM OF MOVEMENT
- DEVELOPMENT OF BALANCE, COORDINATION, AND MUSCLE STRENGTH
- THRILL OF PHYSICAL CHALLENGE
- DEVELOPMENT OF ROLE PLAY AND IMAGINATION
- NONTHREATENING SOCIAL INTERACTION

## Reflections and Ideas for Application

8. Ask parents to meet back in their small groups and exchange handouts with another group. Ask them to address one of the concerns listed on their new handout by suggesting some modifications to the activities so that children could still benefit from them.

9. Return each group's original handout and discuss the suggestions made.

## Follow-up Plans

10. Ask parents to think about their own households, the interests and physical needs of their children, and their own energy levels. Then ask them to find a partner and answer the two questions written on Chart 17B. Feature some of these responses on the parent bulletin board.

**Chart 17B—Use in Step #10**

- WHICH OF THE INDOOR ACTIVITIES LISTED ON THE HANDOUT CAN YOU SEE YOURSELF PARTICIPATING IN WITH YOUR CHILD?

- WHAT MATERIALS COULD YOU PROVIDE THAT WOULD EXTEND THE CURRENT PLAY INTERESTS OF YOUR CHILD?

# I Think I Can Live With . . .

Look at the activities below. Talk with your group members about your own comfort level with these kinds of exuberant indoor activities in your household. As you discuss each item, write down some benefits of the activity for your child as well as concerns you might have about allowing your child to do that activity inside.

**Banging and parading** (with musical instruments made out of pots, pans, plastic containers, and wooden spoons)

*Child benefits:*

*Parental concerns:*

**Jumping** (on or from beds, couches, old mattresses, mini-trampolines, indoor climbers)

*Child benefits:*

*Parental concerns:*

● ● ● ▶

**Throwing, tossing, batting, and kicking** (beach balls, beanbags, pillows, balloons)

*Child benefits:*

*Parental concerns:*

**Stacking** (empty boxes, plastic containers, sofa cushions)

*Child benefits:*

*Parental concerns:*

**Dancing and stretching** (with music, streamers, scarves, ballet bar)

*Child benefits:*

*Parental concerns:*

●●● ►

**Sliding** (down the steps on belly or bottom, across the floor in stocking feet or with waxed paper attached to shoes)

*Child benefits:*

*Parental concerns:*

**Riding, swinging, rocking** (wheeled toys, indoor trapeze, swivel chairs, hobbyhorse)

*Child benefits:*

*Parental concerns:*

**Hiding** (spreading sheets over table tops, building tents and forts with couch cushions and pillows, rearranging heavy objects like furniture to make enclosures, removing cupboard or closet contents to fit inside)

*Child benefits:*

*Parental concerns:*

# 18 Understanding Children's Responsibilities Around the House

## Goals

✔ To discuss realistic expectations for preschool-aged children's ability to take care of personal tasks at home

✔ To discuss ways parents might adjust their expectations so children can feel successful when taking part in responsibilities at home

## Materials

- Chart pad and markers or overhead projector
- Opening activity worksheet titled "Test Your Responsibility Quotient"
- Handout titled "What Can I Realistically Expect My Child to Do?"
- Charts 18A and 18B (prepared ahead of time on a large piece of chart paper or an overhead transparency)

## Introduction

1. Tell parents that tonight you will be looking at the types of personal responsibilities young children can handle and how parents can help children be successful in carrying them out.

## Opening Activity

2. Ask parents to individually fill out the "Test Your Responsibility Quotient" worksheet.

3. As a whole group, ask parents to speculate on the reasons you asked them to do this exercise and what it might have to do with their children. Record their responses on chart paper. Be sure to reinforce points like the following:

- It's hard for anyone—adult or child—to maintain high standards and be perfect all the time.
- Unreasonably high expectations of behavior can be discouraging and frustrating for both children and parents.

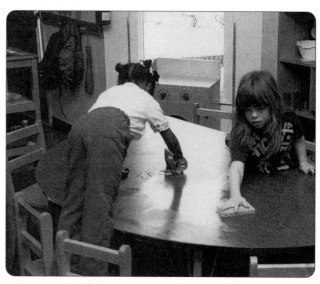

*Sharing with parents the tasks children do in the classroom helps to illustrate the types of responsibilities children can handle at home.*

- For young children, responsibility doesn't necessarily involve putting away all their clothes or changing the bed sheets; simpler tasks might be more appropriate.

### Central Ideas

4. Emphasize the importance of establishing realistic, age-appropriate expectations for young children's responsibilities at home. Point out that these responsibilities should start out simple for preschoolers and gradually become more complex as children grow and mature.

5. Have parents divide into groups of three or four each. Pass out the "What Can I Realistically Expect My Child to Do?" handout and ask parents to follow the directions.

6. Meet back as a whole group and ask parents to report some of their conclusions. If necessary, challenge parents to think of ways to simplify

---

### Chart 18A—Use in Step #6
PARENTING STYLES THAT . . .

#### Support

- OBSERVING WAYS CHILDREN TAKE RESPONSIBILITY AND ENCOURAGING THEM TO CONTINUE

- SIMPLIFYING TASKS SO CHILDREN CAN BE SUCCESSFUL

- ALLOWING PLENTY OF TIME FOR CHILDREN TO COMPLETE TASKS

- RECOGNIZING AND ACKNOWLEDGING CHILDREN'S EFFORTS

#### Hinder

- DISCOURAGING CHILDREN FROM HELPING BECAUSE THEY WON'T DO IT AS WELL AS YOU OR BECAUSE YOU CAN DO IT FASTER

- LECTURING CHILDREN ON THE PROPER WAY TO TIE THEIR SHOES, BRUSH THEIR TEETH, AND PUT AWAY THEIR TOYS

- NAGGING CHILDREN TO HURRY WITH TASKS, EMPHASIZING THE END RESULT MORE THAN THE PROCESS

- CRITICIZING CHILDREN FOR WHAT THEY <u>CAN'T</u> DO

some of the items they have suggested. For example, if a group lists *putting on own sneakers* under the personal hygiene section, ask parents which other parts of this task might be possible for children who have not yet mastered tying their shoelaces.

## Reflections and Ideas for Application

7. Display Chart 18A. Go through each of the points listed, giving parents time to comment and ask questions.

8. Ask parents to work in their small groups and list one example for each of the *support* and *hinder* statements listed on Chart 18A. When they have finished, ask each group to share one example.

## Follow-up Plans

9. Before ending the meeting, ask parents to make a plan for using the information at home by completing the two statements on Chart 18B. Tell them that they may do this activity privately or discuss it with another person, as they prefer.

> **Chart 18B—Use in Step #8**
> • ONE EXAMPLE OF A SUPPORTIVE PARENTING STYLE THAT I WILL TRY AT HOME IS . . .
> • ONE EXAMPLE OF A HINDERING PARENTING STYLE THAT I WILL MAKE AN EFFORT TO STOP USING IS . . .

10. Observe the various ways in which children take responsibility in the classroom. Jot down your anecdotes on the parent bulletin board, making sure to include all children.

# Test Your Responsibility Quotient

Please answer the following 10 questions as they apply to *you* rather than to your child. Place a T for true or an F for false in the space provided. Responses will be confidential, so please answer honestly. Your answers will guide the discussion that will follow.

1. _____ I never leave my work or casual clothes on a chair or on top of my bed after changing outfits. I always put them back in the closet or drawers, or in the hamper when they are dirty.

2. _____ I make my bed every morning after waking, and change my sheets at least twice a month.

3. _____ I always wash my hands thoroughly after each bathroom visit.

4. _____ At home or in a restaurant, I eat all of the food offered to me, even when I don't like it.

5. _____ I never have urges to splash in a rain puddle, make a snow angel, or put my toes and fingers in wet sand.

6. _____ The contents of my kitchen cabinets and pantry are orderly and neat.

7. _____ I can always easily find a screwdriver, a hammer, or pen and paper when I need them.

8. _____ If you were to open my sock drawer right now, you would see only pairs of socks—no single ones waiting to find a match.

9. _____ I have never participated in a food fight, smashed cake into someone's face, or thrown spaghetti at the wall to test for doneness.

10. _____ As soon as I am finished eating, I always clear the dishes from the table, wash and dry them, and put them away before moving on the next activity.

**HANDOUT**

# What Can I Realistically Expect My Child to Do?

Read through the list of household responsibilities and discuss some ways preschool-aged children might be able to participate in them. Write your suggestions in the space provided. The first item is completed for you. (Note that although you will list a variety of ways children *could* participate, you would not expect children to do all the things on the list at one time.)

*Cleaning up after dinner:*

BRING PLASTIC BOWLS OR SILVERWARE TO THE SINK.

WIPE OFF THE TABLE (AFTER THE DISHES HAVE BEEN CLEARED) WITH A DAMP SPONGE.

PUSH THE CHAIRS IN AROUND THE TABLE.

THROW PAPER NAPKINS INTO THE WASTEBASKET.

CLEAN SMALL AREAS WITH A HAND VACUUM OR A SMALL WHISKBROOM AND PAN.

*Getting dressed before school:*

*Taking care of personal hygiene (bathing, brushing teeth, washing hair, toileting):*

*Putting away toys:*

# IV.
# Adult-Child
# Interaction

# 19 Power Struggles at Home

## Goals

✔ To discuss typical parent-child interactions during difficult situations

✔ To offer positive interaction strategies to use in these situations

## Materials

- Pre-made name tags placed in certain spots around small-group tables
- Chart 19A (prepared ahead of time on a large piece of chart paper or an overhead transparency)
- Handouts: "Positive Adult-Child Interaction Strategies for Difficult Situations" "Morning, Dinner, and Bedtime Dilemmas"
- Chart pad and marker or overhead projector
- Pencils and pens for each small-group table
- Paper and markers

## Introduction

1. Greet parents individually as they arrive, and tell them that the meeting will start promptly in 5 minutes. Direct them to their assigned seats, and tell them to wait quietly while you prepare a few last-minute things. If they move their name tag to a different seat, say "Excuse me, but I put that there for a specific reason, and I have to ask you to go back to where it was."

2. Bustle around the room, placing pens and pencils on each table, setting up the refreshment table, and moving the chart pad easel or overhead projector into place at the front of the room (making sure Chart 19A is not visible to parents). If anyone tries to draw you into a conversation, say "I'm sorry, but this is not a good time. I have too much to get ready." If anyone offers to help, politely but firmly tell them "No, please

*Looking at issues from the child's point of view in addition to one's own often aids in finding a solution to stressful situations.*

go back to your seat. Right now the biggest help would be for everyone to just sit quietly."

### Opening Activity

3. Go to the front of the room, stand next to the easel or overhead projector and say "OK, let's get started. This is an important topic and we have a lot to cover, so I need everyone's attention." Then show Chart 19A to the group.

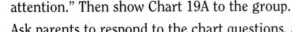

**Chart 19A—Use in Step #3**

- WHEN YOU TOLD ME TO SIT QUIETLY IN AN ALREADY ASSIGNED SEAT, I . . .
- WHEN YOU WOULDN'T RESPOND TO MY QUESTION OR COMMENT, I . . .
- WHEN YOU REJECTED MY OFFER TO HELP, I . . .

4. Ask parents to respond to the chart questions, and record the phrases and key words they use. You may hear answers like these: "I got mad because I could have made the coffee, but you wouldn't let me." "I thought you were too bossy." "I felt unappreciated and unnoticed."

### Central Ideas

5. Agree with parents that when one person retains all the control in a situation or neglects to acknowledge the strengths of another person *(Sit down. Go to your assigned seat. Don't help me.)* feelings of anger, rejection, and helplessness can disrupt the learning experience. Tell parents that in this meeting you will look at two strategies adults can use during disagreements or difficult situations to avoid making others feel as they felt during the opening activity. Tell them that you will discuss these strategies first in relation to the opening activity and then in relation to situations with their own children.

6. Pass out the handout titled "Positive Adult-Child Interaction Strategies for Difficult Situations." As a whole group, make connections between the feelings expressed by parents in the opening activity and the points listed on the handout. Ask parents to identify ways that your actions before the meeting did not demonstrate *sharing control* and *focusing on the strengths of others.* Then ask for suggestions on how you might have used these strategies and how the outcome might have been different.

### Reflections and Ideas for Application

7. Tell parents that next you are going to look at using these interactional strategies in situations that commonly come up between parents and children. Pass out the handout titled "Morning, Dinner, and Bedtime Dilemmas." Read through the first dilemma together, and discuss how the proposed solution helps the child share control and/or focuses on her particular strengths.

8. Dividing into small groups of five or six, ask parents to spend the next 15 minutes completing the rest of the handout. Have each group share one

thought from their discussion. Record these on chart paper or an overhead transparency.

## Follow-up Plans

9. Alone or with a partner, have parents look at the points under the two inter-action strategies and write down on a separate piece of paper a specific situation when they might consider allowing their children some control.

10. Collect the plans parents write down from Step #9 and compile them in a list to post on the parent bulletin board. As parents pick up and drop off their children, encourage them to add anecdotes and suggestions.

**HANDOUT**

# Positive Adult-Child Interaction Strategies for Difficult Situations

## Share Control With Children

- Listen to what your child is **really** saying and acknowledge it.
- Share in the interests of your child.
- Choose times when you can give some control to your child.

## Focus on Your Child's Strengths

- Take a moment to look at the situation from your child's perspective.
- Offer your child choices based on what he or she likes to do and does well.

# Morning, Dinner, and Bedtime Dilemmas

Read the scenarios below. Choose one of the dilemmas to work on as a group, or make up a new one. Use the strategies listed on the "Positive Adult-Child Interaction Strategies" handout to guide you in discussing the dilemma. List your group's comments in the space provided.

## Morning Dilemma

You need to leave the house in 20 minutes to get your daughter to school on time. She is in her bedroom playing with her toys. You called her to the breakfast table 10 minutes ago, but she insists she is not hungry and doesn't want to eat anything.

*Problem:*

YOU FEEL YOUR CHILD NEEDS TO EAT BEFORE SHE GOES TO SCHOOL, BUT SHE REFUSES.

*Possible solution:*

SAY TO YOUR DAUGHTER "YOU MIGHT NOT FEEL HUNGRY RIGHT NOW, SO YOU DON'T FEEL LIKE EATING." THEN OFFER AN ALTERNATIVE: "I'LL BRING A BANANA AND SOME CRACKERS IN THE CAR IN CASE YOU CHANGE YOUR MIND."

## Dinner Dilemma

It is important to you that your family sit down together to eat a meal in the evening. The food is ready, but your 4-year-old son is asking if he can eat his meal while he watches his favorite video.

*Problem:*

•••▶

*Possible solutions:*

## Bedtime Dilemma

Lately your 5-year-old daughter has been getting up after she is already in bed for the night. She opens the door to her room and says she's still not tired. You have tried putting her back in her bed, but she persistently gets out. She does fall asleep if you lie on the bed with her. Some nights it only takes 5 minutes, but other nights it takes 20.

*Problem:*

*Possible solutions:*

# 20 Understanding and Dealing Effectively With Children's Outbursts

## Goals

✔ To look at children's loss of control from the perspective of both parents and children

✔ To practice using supportive strategies to help children through outbursts and emotionally difficult moments

## Materials

- Chart pad and markers or overhead projector
- Handouts: "When My Child Does _____, I Feel _____"
             "Adult Support Strategies to Use When Children Lose Control"
- Pencils and pens for each small-group table

## Introduction

1. Ask parents if they have ever witnessed someone else's child having an outburst in a park, grocery store, or toy store. Tell parents that you will be looking tonight at common situations that create strong feelings and reactions in both parents and children. Explain that you will also discuss ways parents can effectively use active learning and support strategies during these situations.

## Opening Activity

2. Pass out the worksheet titled "When My Child Does _____, I Feel _____." Ask parents to work in small groups of three or four and follow the directions on the handout. Give them 10 minutes to discuss the scenarios.

## Central Ideas

3. Bring the whole group back together. Ask parents to identify some of the feelings they discussed for each scenario; record these on a piece of chart paper or an overhead transparency titled "Parental Feelings." Words to expect include *embarrassed, angry, annoyed.* As parents describe their

feelings, be sure to listen carefully and acknowledge their responses. (For example, "It *is* embarrassing when a child screams in a store. You feel like everyone is looking at you.")

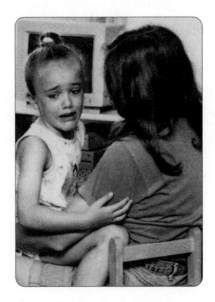

4. In their small groups, have parents return to the worksheet, this time discussing the scenarios from the perspective of the child involved. After they have identified what the child in each scenario may be feeling, come back as a whole group and list these feeling words on a chart titled "Children's Feelings." Expect the list to be similar to the feelings parents said *they* would feel.

5. Ask the group what can be learned from looking at these situations from both points of view. Be sure to make the point that although children experience strong feelings in these situations just as adults do, children often express their emotions in an outburst because they do not yet have the maturity to express themselves more calmly.

*There are often a variety of feelings behind children's outbursts— frustration, anger, fear, jealousy.*

## Reflections and Ideas for Application

6. Pass out the handout titled "Adult Support Strategies to Use When Children Lose Control." Ask parents to choose one of the opening activity scenarios, read through each of the six strategies on the handout, and discuss how they might apply to their selected scenario.

7. As a whole group, ask parents to share how they think the recommended strategies would help them in future situations when their own children have an outburst.

## Follow-up Plans

8. Put a "Difficult Situations" box near the entranceway to the classroom. Ask parents to write down and place in the box a description of a time when their children had an outburst, as well as some of the strategies they used to manage the situation. After you have collected five or six anecdotes, make up a handout to share with parents listing the problems and one or two solutions from parents or from the handout "Adult Support Strategies to Use When Children Lose Control."

# When My Child Does ___ , I Feel ___

Read the following four scenarios that describe some typical behaviors of preschool-aged children. With the members of your group, make a list of all the feelings you might experience if you were the parent in the scenario. Don't worry about what you think you *should* feel; simply record what you think your *true* feelings would be.

## Scenario One

You are having a dinner party for friends at your house. You have been busy the past few days shopping for groceries, preparing the food, and cleaning the house. You expected your 4-year-old daughter to "entertain" your friends' 3-year-old daughter when they arrived, but the moment your friends arrive your daughter runs into her bedroom and closes the door. She comes out about 15 minutes later. She cries when she sees your friends' daughter playing with one of her puzzles on the living room floor and screams, "That's *my* puzzle!"

*Feelings:*

## Scenario Two

You are at the grocery store. Your son reaches from the cart and picks up a candy bar from the display. When you tell him to put it back because he hasn't eaten dinner yet, he begins yelling that he's hungry right now and doesn't want to wait.

*Feelings:*

● ● ▶

## Scenario Three

You pick up your 5-year-old daughter at day care, eager to hear about her field trip to an art studio. Instead, you are greeted by a child who tells you that your daughter "wrote" with ink on the dress of another child while on the field trip and that it made the other child "cry really hard." When you ask your daughter what happened, she tells you that she did it because "her dress is new and prettier than mine."

*Feelings:*

## Scenario Four

You bring the mail in and see your 4-year-old son's invitation to his friend's birthday party. The party is being held at a local pizza place with an indoor gymnasium. Your son jumps up and down and says, "Oh, I love it there!" After telling him he can attend, you remember that you are going out of town that weekend. When you explain to your son that he cannot go to the party, he screams, "I hate you! You never let me do anything fun!"

*Feelings:*

**HANDOUT**

# Adult Support Strategies to Use When Children Lose Control

1. **Try to anticipate problems and plan ahead.** For example, if your shopping trip is going to be a long one, pack a special snack to offer your son before you get to the grocery line, or give him a small toy to hold on to as a replacement for the candy he wants.

2. **Remain calm when your child gets upset.** If your son will let you, comfort him physically (pick him up, rub his back, hold onto his hand). If he is too upset for this, calmly label and validate your child's feelings: "You're really disappointed and angry about missing the pizza party."

3. **Make it clear that while feelings are real, certain behaviors are harmful, dangerous, or inappropriate.** "I know you're jealous of Tanuka's dress, but writing on it ruined her dress and made her feel sad."

4. **Offer alternate ways for your child to express feelings to other children when your child cannot generate ideas independently.** "You're upset that she's playing with your puzzle, but screaming is not OK. Sometimes holding on to your blanket helps you feel better when you're upset."

5. **Involve your child in the solution to the problem.** "Right now you're angry about not being able to go to the party. Maybe we can think of some things to help you feel better."

6. **Understand that your own feelings of anger and embarrassment can make it difficult to remain calm and focused on *long-term solutions* rather than on quick-fix answers.** Find ways to comfort and renew yourself on a regular basis (listening to music, reading the newspaper, taking a jog) so that you will be able to deal with these difficult situations as they arise.

# 21 Solving Everyday Problems: Opportunities for Learning

## Goals

✔ To examine the benefits of solving everyday problems for oneself
✔ To generate a list of common problems preschool-aged children face
✔ To offer a process for parents to use when helping children solve problems

## Materials

- Charts 21A and 21B (prepared ahead of time on a large sheet of chart paper or an overhead transparency)
- Paper and pens/pencils for each small group
- Chart pad and marker
- Handouts: "Common Problems Preschoolers Face"
  "Steps for Supporting Children's Problem Solving"

## Introduction

1. Explain to parents that you will spend the meeting looking at the value of being able to solve problems for oneself, at common problems preschoolers face, and at how parents can support children as they face everyday problems. Stress that you will focus on common problems that individuals experience in the course of a typical day rather than problems that involve conflicts with others. First you will look at situations *parents* might encounter, and then you will examine problems *children* often face.

## Opening Activity

2. Ask parents to divide into groups of four or five each, and give each group a piece of paper and pen or pencil. Display Chart 21A. Ask each group to pick one of the two scenarios on the chart and write down all the possible solutions to the problem.

*When children solve problems on their own—such as getting into a snowsuit—they benefit physically, cognitively, and emotionally.*

**Chart 21A—Use in Step #2**

SCENARIO ONE: YOU DECIDE TO MAKE A QUICK STOP AT THE GROCERY STORE TO PICK UP SOME EGGS AND MILK BEFORE GOING HOME FOR THE EVENING. WHEN YOU GET BACK TO THE CAR AFTER MAKING YOUR PURCHASE, YOU REALIZE YOU HAVE LOCKED YOUR KEYS INSIDE.

SCENARIO TWO: IT IS 11:00 AT NIGHT AND YOU HAVE JUST FINISHED MAKING A SALAD TO TAKE TO A POTLUCK SUPPER TOMORROW. YOUR SINK IS FULL OF APPLE SKINS AND CANTALOUPE RINDS. YOU PUSH IT ALL INTO THE GARBAGE DISPOSAL, TURN ON THE SWITCH, AND NOTHING HAPPENS.

## Central Ideas

3. Give each group a chance to share the solutions they generated. As they list their solutions, focus the discussion on what parents would gain from solving these problems themselves rather than having someone else tell them what to do. Write these benefits on a large piece of chart paper titled "Solving Problems Helps You . . ." Possible benefits drawn from parents' solutions could include the following: *thinking of creative solutions, realizing there is more than one way to do things, drawing on past experiences,* and *thinking critically.*

4. Shifting the focus from parents' situations to children's, pass out the handout titled "Common Problems Preschoolers Face." Ask each small group to read through the handout together and generate additional examples from their own children's experiences.

5. Explain to parents that children as well as adults benefit from being encouraged to solve problems for themselves rather than being given solutions by others. Tell parents that you would like to share five steps that adults can use to assist children when they encounter everyday problems. Pass out the "Steps for Supporting Children's Problem Solving" handout and briefly discuss the process outlined on it.

## Reflections and Ideas for Application

6. Display Chart 21B to parents. Ask small groups to choose one of the scenarios on the chart and apply the steps outlined on the handout to their

Adult-Child Interaction    **123**

scenario. For example, in *Scenario One,* an example of the first step *(Acknowledge the problem and the child's feelings)* might be "Your snow pants won't work. That's kind of frustrating." Ask groups to share their ideas with the whole group, and again focus the discussion on what children gain from the experience of being part of the solution process.

7. Ask parents to look again at the examples they added to the "Common Problems Preschoolers Face" handout. Before ending the meeting, have them work with a partner to choose one of those examples and finish this statement:

   • *The next time this problem arises at home, I will . . .*

> ## Chart 21B—Use in Step #6
>
> <u>SCENARIO ONE:</u> YOU FEEL LIKE IT'S TIME FOR YOUR 4-YEAR-OLD DAUGHTER TO START GETTING HER WINTER CLOTHING ON BEFORE LEAVING FOR SCHOOL EACH MORNING. THIS WOULD GIVE YOU A CHANCE TO PACK THE LUNCHES AND GET YOURSELF A SECOND CUP OF COFFEE. YOU TELL HER TO GO GET DRESSED. TEN MINUTES LATER, SHE COMES INTO THE KITCHEN WITH HER BOOTS ON THE WRONG FEET, HER COAT ON CORRECTLY, AND ONE LEG IN HER SNOW PANTS WITH THE REST OF THE PANTS DRAGGING BEHIND HER. SHE SAYS, "MOMMY, LOOK, IT WON'T WORK!"
>
> <u>SCENARIO TWO:</u> AT THE PARK WITH YOUR 3-YEAR-OLD SON, YOU JUST GET SETTLED ON THE PARK BENCH TO READ THE NEWSPAPER WHEN YOU HEAR HIM CRY OUT FOR YOU TO COME AND HELP. HE HAS STOPPED HALFWAY DOWN THE SLIDE AND IS LOOKING AT THE BOTTOM OF THE SLIDE, WHICH IS STILL WET FROM YESTERDAY'S RAINSTORM.

## Follow-up Plans

8. Post a chart titled "Children *Can* Solve Problems!" on the parent news board. Fill it with pictures of children as they confront and solve problems, or of anecdotes that illustrate these situations. Be sure you include all children and that you highlight what the children are actually learning from the situations.

**HANDOUT**

# Common Problems Preschoolers Face

- Spreading peanut butter on a bagel
- Opening up an individually packaged granola bar
- Putting a straw in a juice box
- Passing out one plate for each family member at dinner
- Turning the faucet on to warm water
- Figuring out which shoe goes on which foot
- Understanding whether snow pants go on *before* or *after* a coat
- Finishing breakfast in time to leave for school
- Pedaling a bike or riding toy up a slight incline
- Putting a sweater on a baby doll or stuffed animal

*Additional problems:*

**HANDOUT**

# Steps for Supporting Children's Problem Solving

1. Acknowledge the problem and your child's feelings.
2. Encourage your child to describe the problem to you.
3. Ask your child for ideas on solutions to the problem.
4. Allow enough time for your child to solve the problem independently.
5. When your child is too frustrated or on the verge of abandoning his or her own ideas, offer your help.

# 22 Feeling Comfortable With Children's Social Bloopers

## Goals

✔ To acknowledge situations when children say and do things in public that embarrass adults

✔ To examine the messages children get from adults' reactions to their behavior

✔ To offer ideas for comforting or supporting children during these times

## Materials

• Handouts: "You Did _____, Then I Did _____, Now You Think _____"
   "On-the-Spot Comfort and Support Strategies"

• Chart pad and marker or overhead projector

## Introduction

1. Tell parents that the focus of this meeting will be on some of the embarrassing things children do and say in public. Explain that the way parents handle these situations can have a positive or negative influence on children. Let parents know that tonight you will offer them some ideas for comforting or supporting children during these situations, as well as ways to help children express their feelings and observations more appropriately.

## Opening Activity

2. Ask parents to recall an embarrassing scene—other than one involving an emotional outburst—they have witnessed between a child and parent in a grocery store, department store, doctor's office, or airport/bus terminal that made them think to themselves, "Glad it's not me this time!" Have them describe the scene to a partner.

## Central Ideas

3. As a whole group, share two or three of the parents' stories. Emphasize that *all* parents experience situations when their children do things that they or other adults around them might find unacceptable. Acknowledge

the discomfort this creates for parents, and tell parents that the next activity will help them understand the effects on *children* when parents react to their behavior in certain ways.

4. Pass out the handout titled "You Did _____, Then I Did _____, Now You Think _____" to each group of four or five people. Ask parents to follow the directions on the handout. Stress that they should fill in the spaces with all possible reactions, even if they personally feel that some of the reactions would be inappropriate.

5. Meet back as a whole group. Discuss which parental reactions generated might inspire messages of understanding, patience, shared problem solving, and empathy for the child's feelings.

## Reflections and Ideas for Application

6. Pass out the "On-the-Spot Comfort and Support Strategies" handout. After parents have read through it, ask them to meet with their partner from the opening activity. Have each team choose one of the scenarios on the handout and practice ways the suggested strategies could be used in that scenario.

7. Meet back as a large group and ask volunteers to share additional examples. Point out how they reinforce the messages of understanding, patience, shared problem solving, or empathy for the feelings of others.

## Follow-up Plans

8. Give parents two suggestions for putting into practice the information they received tonight:

   • *When you see other parents reacting to their children in nonsupportive ways in public settings, mentally rehearse how you could handle the same situation differently.*

   • *Think about strategies to deal with your own discomfort in situations with your child. For example, use humor by laughing afterwards with a spouse, friend, or your own parent about the natural mistakes young children make.*

**HANDOUT**

# You Did _____, Then I Did _____, Now You Think _____

Read the scenarios below. After each one, write down the *feelings* the adult might be experiencing, then possible adult *reactions* to the child in the situation. Finally, write down the *messages* the child might receive from the parent's reaction. In each scenario described, one possible reaction is written for you.

## Scenario One

You take your child to a friend's birthday party. When it is time to blow out the candles on the cake, your child leans over and blows them out before the birthday child has a chance. The birthday child cries, and her mother looks at you and rolls her eyes.

| Parent feelings | Parent reactions | Messages to child |
|---|---|---|
| EMBARRASSMENT | GRAB YOUR CHILD AND SAY "NO CAKE FOR YOU!" | "YOU WERE MEAN AND BAD." |

●●● ▶

## Scenario Two

You take your child to the dentist. When the visit is over, the dentist offers your child a new toothbrush and a pencil. After taking one of each, he pauses for a moment and says, "Can I have some for my little brother, too?"

| Parent feelings | Parent reactions | Messages to child |
|---|---|---|
| UNEASINESS | "NEVER MIND, WE'LL STOP AT THE STORE AND GET YOUR BROTHER HIS OWN." | "DON'T ASK FOR THINGS FROM ADULTS." |

# On-the-Spot Comfort and Support Strategies

Read the scenarios below. Choose one and discuss how the strategies outlined after the scenarios could be used. Some examples are already suggested to help you get started.

## Scenarios

1. You are in the grocery store with your 3-year-old. Your child points to a woman next to you and says in a loud voice, "Mommy, look how fat that lady is!" The woman turns around and says to your child, "You're a rude brat."

2. You invite some friends to your house for dinner. They bring your 4-year-old son a present and after opening it, he says, "This toy is for babies—I'm in *preschool* now."

## Strategies

1. **Do nothing; simply wait.** Sometimes other adults involved in the situation are understanding and patient with young children's behaviors and will handle the situation without your interference.

2. **Resist the urge to yell at or shame children when they say or do things that are uncomfortable for you.** Instead, remain calm, and be matter-of-fact as you address the situation: "Well, people come in all sizes and colors." This type of statement is a description of your child's observations rather than an attack on your child's comment.

3. **Give children information about social rules in a way that makes sense to them.** "You *did* play with toys like this when you were younger, but I'm worried that Stella's feelings were hurt when you said that."

4. **Model more appropriate ways for your child to deal with social situations.** A simple "I'm sorry her words upset you" to the large woman in the grocery store may open the door to later conversations with your child about when and how to talk appropriately about people and things in your environment.

5. **Stick to descriptions when tensions are running high.** "You said something she didn't like, then she said something to you that you didn't like. Lots of people feel sad right now."

# 23 Helping Children Resolve Social Conflicts

## Goals

✔ To identify methods commonly used in solving conflicts with others

✔ To look at social conflict as an opportunity for children to develop problem-solving skills

✔ To offer strategies for parents to help children resolve issues themselves rather than to do it for them or to punish them for immature reactions

## Materials

- Charts 23A and 23B (prepared ahead of time on a large piece of chart paper or an overhead transparency)
- Paper and pens or pencils
- Handouts: "Helping Children Resolve Issues With Others"
          "Applying the Steps for Helping Children Resolve Issues
              With Others"
- Chart pad and markers or overhead projector

## Introduction

1. Tell parents that tonight you will discuss social conflicts that commonly occur among young children. Explain that you will offer parents ways to support children in developing the skills they need to maturely resolve issues, such as taking into consideration their own and other people's perspectives.

## Opening Activity

2. Ask parents to divide into groups of three to four each. Display Chart 23A and give each group a piece of paper and pen or pencil. Ask the groups to choose one scenario on the chart and make a list of possible reactions, without worrying about whether they are positive or negative.

## Central Ideas

3. Ask parents to share with the whole group some of their reactions to the problems on Chart 23A. Write down their responses on chart paper and post it where it can be seen during the next activity.

**Chart 23A—Use in Step #2**

SCENARIO ONE: YOU ARE STUCK IN A TRAFFIC JAM WITH SEEMINGLY NO END TO THE LINE OF CARS AHEAD OF YOU. JUST AS THE TRAFFIC SEEMS TO BE OPENING UP, A CAR COMES RACING UP THE SHOULDER OF THE ROAD AND CUTS IN FRONT OF YOU.

SCENARIO TWO: YOUR NEXT-DOOR NEIGHBOR HAS A GREATER SWISS MOUNTAIN DOG WHO WEIGHS 90 POUNDS. ON SOME MORNINGS, THE DOG GOES OUTSIDE AT 6 A.M. AND IMMEDIATELY WALKS INTO YOUR FRONT YARD AND POOPS ON THE GRASS. IN A RUSH TO GET TO YOUR CAR ONE MORNING, YOU CUT ACROSS THE LAWN AND STEP IN ONE OF THE DOG'S DEPOSITS.

4. Tell parents that they are going to look now at two scenarios depicting common social conflicts between *children*. Ask parents to return to their small groups and discuss ways children might react to the scenarios listed on Chart 23B. Again, ask them to list all possibilities, even those they disapprove of or that make them uncomfortable.

5. As a whole group, discuss similarities and differences between adults' and children's reactions to social conflict. Similarities might include angry reactions (honking the horn, leaving a nasty note, pushing and shoving) or reactions that placate the other person (cleaning up the dog poop without saying anything to the neighbor, giving up the computer game to avoid fighting). Differences might include adults' starting a rational discussion ("Your dog's morning habits create a problem for me that I'd like to talk about") and children's screaming match in the back of the car ("I had it first." "No, *I* had it first!").

6. Summarize this discussion by pointing out that it is not uncommon for both adults and children to react to conflict in immature ways, sometimes without consideration of everyone's needs and perspectives. Stress that mature behavior in conflicts with others is learned through practice and experience.

**Chart 23B—Use in Step #4**

SCENARIO ONE: YOU HAVE JUST PURCHASED A NEW COMPUTER GAME. YOUR TWO CHILDREN BOTH WANT TO PLAY IT ALONE RIGHT AWAY, BUT YOU ONLY HAVE ONE COMPUTER.

SCENARIO TWO: YOU ARE DRIVING IN THE CAR WITH YOUR TWO CHILDREN IN THE BACK SEAT. THERE IS A TOY ON THE SEAT BETWEEN THEM, AND IN THE REAR-VIEW MIRROR YOU SEE THEM BOTH REACHING FOR IT AT THE SAME TIME.

7. Pass out and review together "Helping Children Resolve Issues With Others" handout. Explain that as parents apply the steps on the handout repeatedly in children's conflicts, over time children will develop the skills needed to manage conflict in a positive way.

## Reflections and Ideas for Application

8. Pass out the handout titled "Applying the Steps for Helping Children Resolve Issues With Others." Have parents break into groups of three or four each and follow the directions listed on the handout.

9. Gather back as a whole group and review the answers on the handout. Respond to any questions or comments parents may have. Wrap up the meeting by asking parents to replace the statements below with ones that more closely fit what they have discussed tonight. Do this verbally as a whole group.

   • *"If you don't take turns with that toy, I'm going to take it right back to the store."*

   • *"Since you can't decide who is going first, I'll decide. After 10 minutes, you can switch."*

*Supporting children's efforts to solve their own problems and conflicts, even when it seems easier for parents to solve the disputes themselves, allows children to develop important interactional skills.*

## Follow-up Plans

10. Put a "What Works/What Doesn't Work" box at the entrance of the classroom. Ask parents to try some of the ideas discussed in the meeting and write down the results to put in the box. Use their comments for the topic of a future meeting.

11. Add the *Supporting Children in Resolving Conflicts* videotape* to the parent lending library and encourage parents to check it out to view at home.

12. Display the "Steps in Resolving Conflicts" wall chart* on the parent bulletin board.

---

*These products are available from High/Scope—see p. 182.

**HANDOUT**

# Helping Children Resolve Issues With Others

1. **Approach the conflict in a calm manner.** Nothing escalates an already difficult situation more than a third person who yells, yanks children apart, or otherwise adds to the existing tension.

2. **Stop any hurtful behavior by taking direct action and describing limits to children.** Do this in a firm, matter-of-fact voice without judging or blaming the child: "I see you're mad, but I'm holding your arms because hitting hurts people!" Remember that children's differing interests and personalities will create clashes in the course of their daily play, and that their ability to deal constructively with these strong emotions is just emerging.

3. **Encourage children to talk to one another about the problem.** Ask for and listen to their explanations of the situation. Again, do so without making judgments, even when you feel that one child may be exaggerating the situation. Your job is to remain neutral and let children know that you will listen to all sides. This step will take time and a great deal of patience; however, it will eventually give children a sense of mastery and independence in difficult situations.

4. **Encourage children to take responsibility for their actions, and help them understand that their actions have an impact on other people.** Remember that young children often see only the immediate and only things from their point of view, which makes this step more difficult to accomplish. However, with adult support, children *can* learn to solve problems and trust that adults will be available to help them. They will also learn to be empathic and help other people.

5. **Offer statements that might move a stalemated argument along.** However, resist the temptation to simply solve the problem for the children. Try saying "I can't help but notice that while you are arguing, no on is getting a chance to play with the toy" rather than "Here is another toy; now play with that."

**HANDOUT**

# Applying the Steps for Helping Children Resolve Issues With Others

Read the statements listed below. Match each one with one of the steps outlined in the handout titled "Helping Children Resolve Issues With Others." Write the number of the step your group thinks fits best in the space provided.

A. _____ As the children argue while you are driving, you say, "What's happening back there? You both look upset."

B. _____ As both children are pulling on the new CD-ROM game, you walk over, put your hand on the game, and sit down between them.

C. _____ "Stop pulling on the CD-ROM. It could break the game."

D. _____ "A bump like that needs to have an ice pack held on it for a few minutes."

E. _____ "So, you think she *always* gets things first just because she's older."

# 24 Helping Children Cope With Childhood Losses

## Goals

✔ To look at the different ways young children react to the loss of familiar people, pets, surroundings, and situations

✔ To offer strategies for parents to help children cope with loss

## Materials

• Chart pad and markers

• Handouts: "Facing New Situations"
"Children's Common Reactions to Personal Loss and Ways to Help Them Cope"

## Introduction

1. Explain to parents that this meeting will focus on how childhood losses (death of a pet or a relative, divorce or separation in the family, new parental love interest, moving away from the neighborhood) affect young children. Tell parents that you will also discuss ways they can help children cope with the strong feelings they experience during these situations.

## Opening Activity

2. Ask parents to break up into groups of three or four. Give each group the handout titled "Facing New Situations," and ask them to react to the scenarios presented. Give them 15 minutes to discuss the situations, then bring the whole group back together.

## Central Ideas

3. On a large piece of chart paper, make three columns and label them *My initial feelings, My first reactions,* and *Things that would soothe me.*

4. Fill out the three columns using feedback from each small group. Accept all responses without making any judgments. Responses in the first column might include *stunned, angry,* and *discouraged.* Reactions in the second col-

umn might be *poured a glass of wine, went to sleep early,* and *complained to my spouse.* The third column might list *rented a comedy video, treated myself to a new coffee mug,* and *took my children for a walk in the new neighborhood.*

5. Lead a whole-group discussion about how the chart might look if the scenarios were of a young child experiencing a relocation or the remarriage of one parent. Highlight the similarities and the differences parents point out. Expect the feelings to be similar to those of parents and the reactions to include things like *bed-wetting, difficulty sleeping, increased outbursts.*

6. Pass out the handout titled "Children's Common Reactions to Personal Loss and Ways to Help Them Cope." Give parents a few minutes to read through it, then invite their comments, reactions, and questions. Highlight the ways children's understanding of change and loss differs from adults'.

## Reflections and Ideas for Application

7. Have parents divide into smaller groups. Give each group a large piece of chart paper and markers to record their answers to *one* of the following tasks:

*Children react to loss in different ways. Some may exhibit disruptive behavior; others may become quiet and withdrawn.*

- *List several possible reactions of children to the death of a family pet. List three concrete ways you could support them in appropriately expressing their feelings.*

- *Write down three ways you could explain to your 4-year-old child why you are moving to a new location.*

8. As a whole group, discuss parents' responses.

## Follow-up Plans

9. Start a parent lending library that includes books and pamphlets about helping children deal with loss. Include storybooks parents can read to their child as well as reference books that offer support for parents during a difficult loss. Your local librarian or mental health agency are good resources for developing a list of materials.

**HANDOUT**

# Facing New Situations

Read the scenarios below. With your group members, discuss what might be your initial *feelings* (emotions), first *reactions* (behaviors), and *soothing activities* if you were in the position described.

### Scenario One

You have just moved to a new house 400 miles away from where you grew up and where you raised your 5- and 7-year-old sons. In your new kitchen amid a sea of brown boxes, you unpack the first box to find that the handle on your favorite coffee mug is broken.

*My initial feelings:*

*My first reactions:*

*Things that would soothe me:*

• • • ▶

## Scenario Two

Your mother died 2 years ago and her best friend's husband died 3 months afterward. Your father has just told you that he is planning to ask your mother's best friend to marry him. You were aware that they had been dating, but you did not know that the relationship was so serious. You don't really like this woman, and because it's so soon after the death of your mother you think that your father may just be lonely. He's asking you to stand up for him at the wedding and to plan a small reception after the ceremony.

*My initial feelings:*

*My first reactions:*

*Things that would soothe me:*

**HANDOUT**

# Children's Common Reactions to Personal Loss and Ways to Help Them Cope

## Common Reactions

1. **Children often feel confused, angry, nervous, sad, and/or anxious when faced with a change in their life.** They may be too young to verbalize their feelings, but that does not mean they don't experience them. Some children may express their feelings through disruptive behaviors like writing on the wall with crayons, crying when they are dropped off at school when previously they were excited to go, or wetting their bed at night and soiling their clothing during the day. Other children may become extremely quiet, passive, and withdrawn from participation in everyday routines.

2. **Because of their limited understanding, young children do not perceive events in the same way adults do.** For example, children between the ages of 3 and 6 often view death as reversible or think that a deceased pet or person is merely sleeping.

3. **Young children take what adults say literally.** If a divorce is explained to a child as "Daddy went away on a long trip," the child might wonder why Daddy didn't take him along.

4. **Children often feel that their words, and even their thoughts, can magically make things happen.** Be prepared for a young child to think that it must be *her* fault that Daddy left, because one time she was so mad at him she screamed, "I hate you! Go away!" You may need to reassure your child that the situation is not her fault.

## Ways to Help Children Cope

1. **Allow children to relive experiences and express their feelings through play.** Materials for imagining and pretending—such as puppets, dolls, expressive art materials like markers and clay, and building materials like blocks and people figures—offer a way for children to express their loss without having to verbalize it. As they play, observe closely for signs of anger, confusion, sadness, guilt, and grief. Acknowledge and describe these feelings for children as they surface.

•••▶

2. **Be completely honest, yet state things simply.** Avoid saying things like "Trotter (the dog) is just sleeping," or "Daddy is taking a long trip and will be back later." Instead, say "Trotter died—he got very, very old and his heart stopped beating," or "Daddy went far away to live somewhere else, so we won't see him as much as we used to. It will be hard not to have him here."

3. **When possible, prevent or reduce stress by preparing children for a change, asking them for ideas that will help make things easier.** For example, if a child's best friend is moving away, count down the days left on a picture calendar and ask for your child's ideas on how they might spend the last few days together (renting a favorite video and eating popcorn, going to a special park, or painting a picture the other child can take along).

4. **Be as concrete as possible to keep the lines of communication open for children who want to talk about the people or things that are gone.** Look together at photos of the family pet who died or the parent who moved, and listen for your child's comments and reactions. Revisit places you went to together (a favorite restaurant, a park where you played Frisbee with the dog), and casually start a conversation like "Remember that day we ate here and Daddy spilled a whole glass of water on his food?" Continue the conversation if your child seems inclined to do so.

5. **Be caring and responsive to your child's feelings, but do not project your *own* feelings onto the child.** Acknowledge that something big has happened in the child's life, but don't make assumptions about what he or she is feeling.

6. **When necessary, set appropriate limits for a child's behavior and offer a socially acceptable outlet for expressing feelings.** "I know you're upset that Daddy left, but these crayon marks on the walls are very hard to clean. You can use this big piece of paper to write on or draw a picture on instead."

V.
Special
Topics

# Traveling With Children

## Goals

✔ To help parents realize that children's and adults' travel needs and interests are different

✔ To help parents balance their own needs with their children's needs during travel

## Materials

- Handouts: "Traveling With Young Children"
  "Travel Plans That Fall Apart"
  "Vacation Plan"

## Introduction

1. Explain to parents that you will be discussing how to plan family travel in a way that meets the needs and interests of both adults and children.

## Opening Activity

2. In groups of two or three, have parents share their positive memories of traveling as children.

3. Make a list of highlights shared by parents. Things to expect might include *spending more time with family, staying up past dark, eating more junk food, getting new toys, putting money in the candy machine at a rest stop, singing in the car, doing new things, buying souvenirs.*

## Central Ideas

4. As a whole group, discuss travel highlights and interests of parents now that they are adults, then point out the differences between *children's* and *parents'* perceptions of travel. Explain to parents that the differing and often competing needs of parents and children while traveling will necessitate

compromises. For example, although parents may not be able to relax with an entire novel during the trip because the children need attention, they may be able to enjoy a shorter magazine article.

5. Pass out the handout titled "Traveling With Young Children" and ask parents to read it in small groups. Have them discuss how the tips might have helped on a past trip or could help on a future trip. Share some of their ideas with the whole group.

## Reflections and Ideas for Application

6. Give each small group the handout titled "Travel Plans That Fall Apart," and ask them to follow the directions written on it. Then discuss each group's recommendations as a whole group.

## Follow-up Plans

7. Give parents the handout titled "Vacation Plan" to take home and fill out before an upcoming trip. Ask for feedback from those who use the handout.

8. Make up several backpacks or prop boxes that parents can borrow to take with them on an upcoming trip. Include materials like paper and markers, tiny containers of play dough, donated cameras and binoculars, and storybooks and puppets. Have a sign-up sheet available, and replenish consumable items when the kits come back from a trip.

9. Create a resource file of brochures and maps of places—especially relatively local ones—where parents have had successful outings with their young children. This will give parents who are planning a trip some "tried-and-true" ideas.

10. Provide a spot on the parent bulletin board for parents to jot down their favorite family vacation memory.

# Traveling With Young Children

## Considerations

1. **Young children think about things in very concrete terms.** To you, a camping trip might mean an opportunity to exercise, breathe some fresh air, and get away from telephones, television, and the hectic pace of your work life. Young children, however, are more likely to focus on interesting things they can explore—such as sticks, stones, and firewood.

2. **Young children are still quite self-centered and unable to see beyond the immediate.** A 4-hour drive to see a national monument makes sense to you as an adult, but don't expect children to share your interest in the historical significance of the site or to sit passively on the way there.

3. **Young children struggle for a sense of control over their environment.** A consistent routine is one way children feel as though they some have control, so any change in their routine may upset them. Therefore, while *you* may be able to give up phones and TV for a week, don't be surprised if your child, who is used to watching a video before bed or playing a computer game while you cook supper, has difficulty dealing with the changes.

## Tips

1. **To help your child understand what to expect on your trip, act out some of the aspects together beforehand.** For example, setting up a tent for an overnight backyard experience will help prepare children for a camping trip, and bringing out lanterns, camping stoves, and sleeping bags will familiarize children with the new ways they will be doing things while camping. Also, expect that children will want to re-enact aspects of the trip afterwards, and encourage them in this.

2. **Plan ways for your child to stay actively involved in as many aspects of the trip as possible.** Have your child help with the preparations by picking out favorite toys and storybooks to pack. If you are traveling by car, plan rest breaks where your child can be physically active. For example, play ball, throw a Frisbee, or take a short walk at a rest area before you plan to sit down and eat a restaurant meal.

3. **As much as possible, follow a routine that is familiar to your child, and allow him or her to have a say in what you do.** For example, plan activities around your child's normal eating and nap times, and let your child choose from suggested options which restaurant to eat at or which camp meal you will cook for supper.

4. **When planning activities that are important to *you*, consider ways to keep your child interested.** If visiting a national monument is part of the plan, for instance, give your child a pair of plastic or toilet-paper-roll binoculars just as you arrive at the overlook. This should interest your child long enough for you to enjoy a few uninterrupted moments to yourself.

**HANDOUT**

# Travel Plans That Fall Apart

Read the following two scenarios. For each one, discuss and record how children's interests, their developmental abilities, or the wishes of the adult influenced the situation. Decide on at least one solution for each scenario.

## Scenario One

You decide to take your 4- and 6-year-old children to Disney World for a 3-day vacation. After the first day, you wonder whether you should cancel the remainder of your trip! The 6-year-old held up well, but your 4-year-old son clung to your legs and cried whenever a Disney character was nearby. He was scared of the rides and didn't like the hot dog you got for lunch because it didn't "taste like the ones at home." On top of that he fell asleep in the stroller for an hour (although he hasn't taken a nap for 6 months), which made it hard to keep up with your other child, who wanted to see everything and go everywhere.

*Discussion points:*

*Possible solutions:*

• • ● ▶

### Scenario Two

You decide to visit your parents for a 1-week family vacation. To avoid the 600-mile drive, you make reservations to fly. Your 3-year-old daughter is fascinated by the airport, especially the moving walkways and the large windows where she can watch the planes loading and taking off. You have timed the flight to coincide with her normal nap schedule, so when you board the plane she settles in and falls right to sleep. Anticipating a short 90-minute flight, you have on board with you only a novel for yourself and your daughter's stroller, favorite storybook, stuffed animal, and blanket. Ten minutes after you board, the captain announces that due to mechanical problems there will be a delay, and passengers should remain seated until further information is available. When you finally get off the plane 3 hours later, you and your daughter are tired, hungry, and extremely irritable.

*Discussion points:*

*Possible solutions:*

# Vacation Plan

Child's name:

Name three things that most interest this child:

Plan two ways these interests could be met while traveling in a car, or on a plane or train:

Name one item of interest that *you* do not want to miss out on during this trip:

Plan two ways to fulfill your own interest while at the same time meeting your child's developmental needs:

# 26 Are Open-Ended Toys Better Than Battery-Operated Ones?

## Goals

✔ To examine the value of a variety of toys
✔ To give parents a guide for evaluating different kinds of toys for preschoolers

## Materials

- A variety of open-ended toys, such as table-top blocks; dolls and stuffed animals; paper and writing instruments; stones, pebbles, rocks, and paper cups; paper clips in different shapes; string; balls; and dress-up clothing
- A variety of battery-operated toys, such as hand-held video games, vehicles, flashlights, alphabet and number board games, cassette tape player and tapes
- Paper and pencils
- Chart pad and markers or overhead projector
- Large sheets of paper divided into two columns, one sheet for each group of four to five parents
- Handout titled "Questions to Consider When Toy Shopping"
- Pictures of battery-operated and open-ended toys (from newspaper advertisements or toy catalogs)
- Glue or tape

## Introduction

1. Tell parents that tonight you will be comparing a variety of toys in terms of the learning opportunities they present for children. Explain that you will also present factors for parents to consider when choosing toys for their children.

## Opening Activity

2. Ask parents to break up into groups of five or six each, and give each group a large sheet of chart paper and a marker. Have them describe their favorite childhood toy to the others in their group and record these on the chart paper.

3. As a whole group, look at each group's list of toys. Then ask parents about their *children's* favorite toys, and record these on a separate sheet of chart paper. Compare the two lists, especially in terms of the number of battery-operated or electronic toys.

## Central Ideas

4. Break into small groups again, and have each group select a recorder to write a short description of what the group members do in the activity that will follow. Give a few examples of what they might observe, such as *lined pebbles in a straight row; took batteries out of tape recorder;* or *said, "Wow, flashlights. If it was night, we could play tag."* Pass out paper and pencils to the recorders.

5. Give each group a bag of toys from the list under *Materials,* making sure that some groups have open-ended toy options while others have battery-operated toys. Tell parents that they have 10 minutes to simply use the materials in any way they like. Remind the recorder to briefly write what the others do with the materials or say about them.

6. Meet back as a whole group, and ask recorders to read some of the observations they made as parents were playing. As they read their statements, write them down on chart paper in the context of the key experiences or your own curriculum goals. For example, if the recorder reports that a parent "flashed the flashlight on the ceiling, the floor, and back and forth and up and down on the wall," you could write down *experiencing light in a variety of classroom spaces.* If the recorder says a parent "put pebbles in one cup and rocks in another," you might write *sorting materials into piles.*

7. Summarize by saying that both open-ended and battery-operated toys can offer learning opportunities for children when used in creative, exploratory, and problem-solving ways. By watching children's behavior as they play, parents will get a better idea of a toy's value and usefulness and can then encourage children to play with a variety of toys.

## Reflections and Ideas for Application

8. Pass out the handout titled "Questions to Consider When Toy Shopping." Have parents break into groups of four or five. Give each group a large sheet of paper with two columns. Have them tape or paste a picture of a battery-operated toy at the top of one column and a picture of an open-ended toy at the top of the second column. Ask them to apply the questions on the handout to both toys and record their responses in the appropriate columns on the chart paper. Give parents time to walk around and read other groups' comments.

*Providing a wide variety of toys—open-ended as well as battery-operated—offers greater possibilities for children's play.*

## Follow-up Plans

9. On the parent news board, display several advertisements for additional toys. Invite parents to comment on them by filling out a nearby sheet of paper or wipe-off board that reads "I would buy this toy because _____" and "I would not buy this toy because _____."

# Questions to Consider When Toy Shopping

1. Why would this toy appeal to my child (or another child I might be buying it for)?

2. List several ways this toy could be used.

3. What kinds of learning opportunities does this toy offer?

4. How safe and durable is this toy?

# 27 Seeing Children in a Positive Light

## Goals

✔ To help parents understand the effects of using negative words to label children
✔ To introduce positive descriptors that can replace negative labels
✔ To give parents a chance to express a positive view of their children

## Materials

• Chart pad and markers or overhead projector
• One bag of materials for each small group. Each bag should include newspaper, masking tape, straws, toothpicks, and a golf ball.
• Two sets of index cards (see the *Opening Activity*), for assigning each participant a role
• Handout titled "A Positive Outlook—A Different Perspective"

## Introduction

1. Explain to parents that the discussion tonight will highlight the importance of viewing and describing children's behavior in a positive rather than negative light.

## Opening Activity

2. Break the group into smaller groups of four to five people each. Give each group a bag of materials (described above) and tell them that they are to construct a bridge strong enough to roll the golf ball across without collapsing. Tell them they will have two chances to construct the bridge. Before they begin, assign each person in the group a role to play during the activity, asking them not to reveal their roles until both structures are completed. Each role, defined below, should be written on an index card.

A. Act BOSSY: Tell the others what your ideas are and why they will work well.

B. Be UNFOCUSED: Play with the materials instead of staying on task.

C. Be SHY: Participate only when others ask you to do something.

D. Act CONFUSED: Question the way others are doing things as though you don't understand.

E. Be CRITICAL: Find fault with other people's ideas and give reasons why they won't work.

3. Have parents break into new groups. Repeat the activity, giving each member in every group a card listing one of the roles below. Be sure to give parents the same lettered card they had the first time; for example, *Parent A* in the first round should be *Parent A* the second time. Cards for this round should read:

A. Be a LEADER: Suggest ideas and explain why you think they will work.

B. Be CREATIVE: Use the materials in the bag in new and different ways.

C. Be WATCHFUL AND OBSERVANT: Join in when asked.

D. Be THOUGHTFUL: Ask others to clarify what they are doing.

E. Be a PROBLEM SOLVER: Question the way others are doing things and explain why it might not work.

### Central Ideas

4. Meet again as a whole group. Ask parents to compare the two roles they played, emphasizing the way different labels affected individuals as well as the group. Write parents' comments on a piece of chart paper.

5. Help parents make a connection between the comments they made in Step #4 and the way children might feel when adults place negative labels on their thoughts, actions, and behaviors. Encourage parents to comment by

*The opening activity described in this workshop demonstrates to parents how positive and negative labels affect their view of themselves and others.*

posing the question "How do you think your children might feel and react when they hear adults call them bossy, hyper, shy, dumb, or whiny?"

6. Pass out the handout titled "A Positive Outlook—A Different Perspective." Ask parents to complete the handout in groups of three or four, following the written directions. When they have finished, bring the whole group back together and address comments or concerns.

## Reflections and Ideas for Application

7. Ask parents to find a partner, possibly a spouse or significant other. Ask them to think back to a situation when their own child was described (or thought about) negatively. Discuss this situation with your partner and brainstorm other, more positive words that could have been used to describe your child.

8. Before leaving, have parents choose one of the positive descriptors listed at the end of the handout that applies to their own child. Ask them to view their child's behavior in light of this descriptor throughout the next week.

## Follow-up Plans

9. During the week following the meeting, ask parents to write down brief observations about the effect that this more positive "label" has had on their view of their children. Post their comments on the parent news board.

# A Positive Outlook—
# A Different Perspective

Read the scenarios listed below. Underline the labels that prejudice adults'
view of children and limit children's belief in their own abilities and strengths.
Replace each label with a positive description of the child's strength. A list
of replacement words that are positive, specific, and descriptive is presented
at the end of the scenarios.

## Scenarios

*A preschool teacher to a father picking up his daughter:* "She's such a rowdy
little girl. I expect that from boys, but girls are usually a little bit more reserved
than she is."

*A pediatrician to a parent concerned about her child's behavior in church:* "You
have to understand that he is hyperactive—you can't expect him to sit for a long
period of time like adults."

*A parent to his son's child care provider:* "You'll have to keep your eye on him.
He's so aggressive with his new baby sister that his mother and I are worried he'll
start hitting the smaller children at school, too."

*A stranger to a parent in a crowded elevator at the public library:* "Boy, what a
whiner. You must really have your hands full."

*Your child's preschool teacher to the whole group of children at morning
circle time:* "Everybody, look at Brianna. She's showing me she's ready for
kindergarten, sitting so quietly and politely."

• • • ▶

## Suggested Replacement Descriptors

- Thoughtful listener
- Careful observer
- Problem solver
- Physically active
- Risk taker
- Enthusiastic
- Persistent
- Verbally expressive
- Curious
- Gives attention to others
- Expresses strong emotions
- *Additional ideas:*

# 28 Rules—Set in Stone or Open to Family Discussion?

## Goals

✔ To discuss rules and the reasons parents make them

✔ To look at guidelines for establishing rules that make sense for the *whole* family

## Materials

- 3 × 5 index cards, one for each parent
- Chart pad and markers
- Handout titled "Rethinking Rules"
- Chart 28A (prepared ahead of time on a large piece of chart paper or an over-head transparency)

## Introduction

1. Explain to parents that you will look tonight at how rules help a household run smoothly, and that you will also present some guidelines for establishing rules that are understandable to and realistic for young children.

## Opening Activity

2. Give each parent a 3 × 5 index card, and ask them to write down two words that come to mind when they hear the word *rules*. Collect the cards and shuffle them.

3. Have parents break into groups of three or four. Give each group two index cards, a piece of chart paper, and a marker. Ask them to discuss the words listed on the cards they received and to agree on a definition that conveys the meaning of those words. Have them write their definition on the chart paper and hang it up where the other groups can see it. Expect statements like the following: *Rules help children know what to expect. Rules teach respect for the person in charge. Rules teach children about right and wrong. Rules encourage children to be sneaky and figure out ways to break them. Rules help keep children safe.*

## Central Ideas

4. Summarize the definitions parents have written, adding the examples in Step #3 if they are not represented. Point out that rules are often thought of as a way to establish authority and encourage obedience. Explain that you would like to encourage parents to look at rules from a slightly different perspective.

5. Pass out the handout titled "Rethinking Rules." Ask parents to find a partner and follow the directions on the handout.

6. Gather back as a whole group and give parents this definition of a rule: *a policy or guideline established for the safety and well-being of the child and other members of the family.* This type of rule is presented to children in ways that they can understand, keeping in mind that young children are not likely to generalize rules from one situation to another. Then focus the discussion on parents' responses to the fourth question on the "Rethinking Rules" handout.

7. Show parents Chart 28A, "Guidelines for Setting Rules." As you review each idea on the chart, give a concrete example to clarify that point.

## Reflections and Ideas for Application

8. Ask parents to once again divide into groups of three or four. Ask them to think of one rule they would all like to establish in their own households and to discuss how they could apply each of the guidelines on Chart 28A to that rule. For example, if the rule is "Two sweet foods a day," they might apply the guidelines like this:

- *Involve children in making rules:* Ask children when they think the best time to eat their two sweets would be.

- *State rules clearly and positively, giving simple explanations:* "You can have two sweet things so you can still be hungry for healthier foods that will make your body grow better."

- *Demonstrate behaviors you **do** want:* Model healthy eating and limit your *own* intake of sweets.

- *Enforce limits consistently:* "I'm sorry, you already had two sweets—the next thing you eat needs to be something healthy."

- *Use natural consequences and avoid punishments:* When the rule gets broken, express your concern for a healthy body instead of taking away sweets for a whole week. Tell your son

---

**Chart 28A—Use in Step #8**
GUIDELINES FOR SETTING RULES

- KEEP RULES TO A MINIMUM.

- WHEN POSSIBLE, INVOLVE CHILDREN IN MAKING THE RULES.

- STATE RULES CLEARLY AND POSITIVELY, GIVING SIMPLE EXPLANATIONS FOR THEM.

- DEMONSTRATE THROUGH YOUR OWN ACTIONS THE BEHAVIORS YOU WANT FROM YOUR CHILDREN.

- ENFORCE LIMITS CONSISTENTLY.

- RATHER THAN PUNISH MISBEHAVIOR, ALLOW CHILDREN TO EXPERIENCE THE NATURAL CONSEQUENCES OF THEIR ACTIONS.

what could happen if he keeps eating too much junk food; for example, it could make him crabby, give him cavities in his teeth, and cause him to become overweight.

9. Ask each group to share a rule and one of the guidelines they came up with.

### Follow-up Plans

10. With a partner or by themselves, have parents list the rules they currently enforce in their households and choose two that they might rework using the guidelines suggested. Ask them to apply one of the new rules at home and share the resulting experience on the parent bulletin board.

**HANDOUT**

# Rethinking Rules

Think about a rule you had in your own family when you were a child, and write it down next to *childhood rule,* below. When you and your partner are finished writing your rules, discuss and answer together the four questions that follow.

*Childhood rule:*

1. What do you think your family members were trying to accomplish by setting this rule?

2. What safety hazards was the rule designed to avoid?

3. As a child, do you remember feeling like you understood the reason for the rule?

4. As an adult, can you think of a way your family members could have modified circumstances somehow so that the rule would not have been necessary? (For example, instead of not allowing children to eat while watching television, perhaps the family could have scheduled dinner time either before or after a favorite television show.)

# 29 Presenting a United Front: Parental Teamwork*

## Goals

✔ To discuss the importance of working as a family team to address child-rearing needs

✔ To compare non-negotiable and negotiable childrearing practices for children

✔ To give information about effective communication techniques and provide an opportunity to apply these techniques to a particular childrearing issue

## Materials

- Chart pad and marker or overhead projector
- Handouts: "I.Q. Test"

  "Non-Negotiable and Negotiable Practices"

  "Tips for Communicating Effectively With Your Childrearing Partner"

- I.Q. Test answer sheet (one copy for presenter)

## Introduction

1. Tell parents that tonight you will explore how parents and other family members responsible for childrearing can work together effectively.

## Opening Activity

2. Ask parents to work in groups of three to four and complete the handout titled "I.Q. Test" together. Review the exercise as a whole group, and ask parents how working together made the I.Q. test easier to complete. List their responses on a piece of chart paper or an overhead transparency. Some answers to expect include the following: "No one had to do it all by themselves—we supported one another." "Everyone contributed their ideas." "We discussed different answers and then accepted one." "We realized some people are better at certain things than others." "Working together made everyone feel a part of the activity."

---

*When announcing this meeting topic, suggest that parental teams attend together.

## Central Ideas

3. Explain to parents that teamwork can help make many different situations—including childrearing—run more smoothly. Acknowledge that childrearing partners do not always see eye to eye on issues, and that you would like to encourage parents to work through these issues and experience the rewards that come from sharing the childrearing experience.

4. Pass out the handout titled "Non-Negotiable and Negotiable Practices." Point out that the issues presented on the handout often cause disagreements between parental team members. Some partners may feel that a particular childrearing practice is *non-negotiable*—set by adults, with no deviation or chance for children to make choices; other partners may see the same practice as *negotiable*—allowing children some choice within the general guidelines set by adults.

5. Go through the first two issues on the handout (*Bedtime routines* and *Eating*) as a whole group, giving an example of a non-negotiable and negotiable practice for each. For example, a non-negotiable bedtime practice might be *8 P.M.—lights out;* a negotiable bedtime practice might still require the child to go to bed at 8 P.M., but would allow him or her to choose a story to read and to decide whether to turn the night-light on or off.

6. Have parents return to their small groups and discuss the rest of the issues on the handout. After they have finished filling in the columns on the handout, ask groups to share their conclusions.

7. Tell parents you realize that some child care issues are such "hot-button" topics that it can be difficult to reach agreement with their spouses or other childrearing partners. Explain that you will present them with some techniques that will help keep the communication process open and allow them to gain satisfaction from working as a team. Pass out the handout titled "Tips for Communicating Effectively With Your Childrearing Partner." As you share the information, be sure to pause for parents' comments and questions.

## Reflections and Ideas for Application

8. Ask parents to meet with the members of their childrearing teams who are present. Ask them to choose *one* issue from the "Practices" handout that is important to their family, and to tackle it using the communication principles outlined on the "Tips" handout. They should work out a strategy they are all willing to try.

## Follow-up Plans

9. Post the answers generated in Step #4 in the classroom to give parents a chance later to review the negotiable-practice suggestions. Ask each family to select one idea from the list that they had not considered trying with their own child and that all agree would be worth the effort.

**HANDOUT**

# I.Q. Test

Here are some real puzzlers for you! Decipher the hidden meaning of each set of words.

| | | | |
|---|---|---|---|
| **1**<br><br>L E S O D U B<br>**TENNIS** | **2**<br><br>timing  tim ing | **3**<br><br>**JJJ  BBB** | **4**<br><br>1/4 1/4 1/4 1/4 1/4 |
| **5**<br><br>hand<br>hand<br>hand<br>deck | **6**<br><br>e  e  q<br>u  a  l<br>s  m  c | **7**<br><br>goodbye | **8**<br><br>**DR.    DR.** |
| **9**<br><br>dipping | **10**<br><br>fighting | **11**<br><br>S  O  E  S<br>H   W   R | **12**<br><br>GGES  EGSG<br>GEGS  SEGG |
| **13**<br><br>HEAD SHOULDERS<br>ARMS BODY LEGS<br>ANKLES FEET TOES | **14**<br><br>K A N E L | **15**<br><br>a chance n | **16**<br><br>THE END<br>↑ |

From *Still More Games Trainers Play: Experiential Learning Exercises* (p. 131), by Edward E. Scannell and John W. Newstrom, 1994, New York: McGraw-Hill, Inc. Copyright © 1994 McGraw-Hill Companies. Reprinted with permission.

●

**HANDOUT**

# Non-Negotiable and Negotiable Practices

| Child care issue | Non-negotiable practice | Negotiable practice |
|---|---|---|
| *Bedtime routines* | | |
| *Eating* | | |
| *Discipline* | | |
| *Cleaning up toys* | | |
| *Back talk* | | |
| *Family outings* | | |
| *Watching television* | | |
| *Other:* | | |

# Tips for Communicating Effectively With Your Childrearing Partner

1. **Set aside a time to discuss child care issues when your child is not present.** It will be less confusing to a child if each adult is in agreement with a plan and follows through with it consistently.

   *Example:* After hearing your child say that your spouse always puts the night-light on but that you sometimes forget, you and your spouse agree that as part of your daughter's bedtime routine, she can turn on the night-light right before getting into bed. This way, your child knows what is coming and does not have to adjust to a different routine depending on who is putting her to bed.

2. **When sharing information about a child, give an honest and specific description of actual words and actions.**

   *Example:* "The other night Jenny started crying at 2 A.M. She said her room was too dark."

3. **Avoid making statements that will arouse feelings of resentment, hurt, or defensiveness in your childrearing partner.**

   *Example:* A statement like "Just because your mom *said* you had to eat all your food before dessert doesn't mean you really have to" causes resentment and division and takes the focus away from the central issue (how to handle your child's eating sweets). It also confuses the child—remember Tip #1.

4. **Listen carefully to the concerns and perspective of the other adult, restating what you heard to make sure your interpretation is accurate.** Use these statements as a starting point for identifying some solutions to the problem.

   *Example:* "You're really worried about helping our child make healthy choices about the things he eats. I want to make sure he eats well, too, but I don't want to limit his choices *too* much."

5. **When you are having difficulty reaching an agreement, set aside the issue for the moment.** Think back to a previous difficult childrearing issue that you successfully resolved in order to get some insight into the current situation or simply for some reassurance that you *will* be able to work things out.

   *Example:* After a great deal of discussion, your son's diet remains a topic of disagreement between you and your partner. The two of you think back to an earlier issue regarding how much mess to tolerate from your toddler when he fed himself. Your partner recalls that you agreed at that time to put smaller amounts of food at a time on your child's plate until he could handle more without getting so much of it on the floor. The two of you now decide to give your child smaller portions of non-nutritious food but allow him to have them more often.

**HANDOUT**

# I.Q. Test Answer Sheet

1. Mixed doubles tennis
2. Split second timing
3. The birds and the bees
4. Close quarters
5. All hands on deck
6. $E=mc^2$
7. Waving goodbye
8. A paradox
9. Skinny dipping
10. Two black eyes
11. Scattered showers
12. Scrambled eggs
13. Head and shoulders above the rest
14. Twisted ankle
15. An outside chance
16. Beginning of the end

From *Still More Games Trainers Play: Experiential Learning Exercises* (p. 133), by Edward E. Scannell and John W. Newstrom, 1994, New York: McGraw-Hill, Inc. Copyright © 1994 McGraw-Hill Companies. Reprinted with permission.

# 30 When Other Adults Criticize Your Child

## Goals

✔ To look at situations in which children are criticized by adults whose childrearing practices differ from parents'

✔ To discuss how parents in these situations can effectively reassure their children and communicate their childrearing preferences to other adults

## Materials

• Chart pad and markers or overhead projector

• Handouts: "Strategies for Reassuring Your Child"
  "When to Step In, What to Say—*You* Decide"

## Introduction

1. Tell parents that tonight's discussion will involve situations in which children's behavior is criticized by another adult—a grandparent, neighbor, stranger—whose childrearing practices differ from the parents'. In these situations, children may be confused and upset at being criticized, causing parents to feel protective of their children and angry at the other adult. Explain to parents that this workshop will focus on ways to handle these situations in a way that reassures children and also communicates the parents' preferences to other adults.

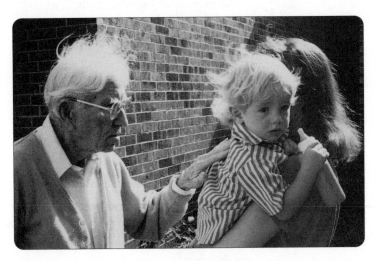

*Family members do not always agree with parents' childrearing practices. Focusing on the confusion that conflicting expectations may cause for children may help to promote cooperation among the adults.*

## Opening Activity

2. Ask parents to divide up and meet with one or two other parents. Have them share one child care issue on which they disagree with their partner, a neighbor, a grandparent, a friend, or their child's teacher. Examples might include the kinds of foods children are allowed to eat, expectations for table behavior, the age at which a child gives up a pacifier, the type of clothes a child wears when attending church, whether to allow a child to swim naked in a backyard wading pool, and how to handle a child's temper tantrum in the grocery store. Ask parents to be specific about the actual comments or nonverbal messages either they or their children have received regarding the particular issue they identify. These might include statements such as "She's too old for that pacifier. It'll ruin her teeth." "Do you just let your kids run around naked all summer?" "You know, my older son has a pair of dressier shoes that might fit your boy."

3. With the whole group, make two charts based on the discussion parents had in Step #2. On the first chart, list the issues parents identified as creating tension for themselves or their children. On the second chart, write the comments or nonverbal messages that parents have received in connection with these issues.

## Central Ideas

4. Acknowledge that these lists contain some real hot-button issues that all families face when raising children in ways that may differ from those of other people around them. Ask parents to work in small groups to choose from these lists those issues they feel are important, for their child's sake, to address with the adults concerned. For example, speaking up to a stranger in the grocery store for a child who sucks her thumb might not be as important as speaking to a grandparent or teacher on behalf of a child who still uses a pacifier.

5. After parents have thought about and identified which issues are central to their own lives, pass out the handout "Strategies for Reassuring Your Child." Review each point with the whole group and encourage parents' comments and questions.

## Reflections and Ideas for Application

6. Pass out the handout titled "When to Step In, What to Say—*You* Decide." Ask parents to meet in small groups and follow the directions written on the handout. When they are finished, ask each small group to share one or two of their ideas with the whole group.

## Follow-up Plans

7. Ask parents to keep an account of situations in which they felt they needed to stand up for their child and times when they successfully did so. Ask them to jot them down on the parent bulletin board.

**HANDOUT**

# Strategies for Reassuring Your Child

1. **Observe closely the reaction of your child to other people's expressed opinions about hot-button issues.** Use these observations to help you decide what the next steps should be for you and your family. For example, if your daughter has been criticized by another adult for sucking a pacifier and she buries her head in your neck, you may just want to cuddle her and stroke her back.

2. **When another person expresses a negative opinion in front of your child, respond directly to your child, being sure to fairly represent all viewpoints.** Do not judge who is right or wrong, good or bad—focus instead on the fact that other people may have different opinions. Use examples of other situations to help your child understand how people can have different viewpoints. For example, you might say something like "Grandma thinks pacifiers should just be for babies, but older children also use them—just like the way some 3-year-olds still wear diapers and some don't."

3. **Have a few responses ready to rely on in surprise situations—responses that address both your child and the person who made the negative comment.** For example, the phrase "Pacifiers can be very comforting, even when children are older" may help you out of an uncomfortable encounter with a stranger in the grocery store line who tells your child she is too old to be sucking one.

4. **Comment on the issue and other people's reactions to the issue, *not* the child's behavior.** An easy way to do this is to describe the behavior and the other adult's reaction in a general way: "You are doing something she doesn't like, and she's telling you what she thinks." This strategy helps to acknowledge both parties without judging either one.

5. **Check back with your child after the moment has passed, and provide ample opportunity for discussion.** Acknowledge and deal with the feelings of all those involved: your child, you, and the other adult.

6. **You may feel it necessary to talk with the other adult about the issue when the child is not present.** In such discussions, remember to *stay calm, acknowledge the other person's opinion,* and *state your own point of view.*

●●● ▶

Emphasize the effect that conflicting expectations have on the child: "I know you think she's too old to suck a pacifier, but it comforts her in new situations. It must be confusing to her to hear such different messages about it."

7. **Recognize that there might be times when the other person's opinions of childrearing practices are so opposed to yours that you have to limit your child's contact with that person.**

**HANDOUT**

# When to Step In, What to Say—*You* Decide

Read the following scenarios. As a group, discuss whether you would stand up for your child in each situation and how you might do so. Write down the specific words you might say in support of your child.

## Scenario One

You are in the elevator of a local library, riding up and down as your daughter plays with the elevator buttons. She is fascinated with pushing the numbers to indicate which floor to stop at. As the door opens, an elderly women gets in. As she raises her cane to push her desired floor number, your 3-year-old child shouts, "Stop! I'll do it!" The woman turns around, leans down, and says, "You're a brat. I used to be a schoolteacher and you're a brat." Your child moves closer to you and wraps her arms around your leg. Everyone else in the elevator is silent.

*Supportive words:*

## Scenario Two

You pick up your 4-year-old son at his child care center earlier than expected. It is nap time and he is sitting on his hands on a chair next to his cot. He starts to cry when he sees you and tells you that his teacher makes him "sit on his hands until they hurt and get cold." Your son often sucks his thumb while settling down to sleep, and you wonder if he is being punished for this.

*Supportive words:*

### Scenario Three

You are celebrating a special meal with extended family members at your mother's home. Your 5-year-old daughter has eaten only a small portion of the food on her plate. When the dessert is brought to the table, your mother says to your daughter, "You can't have a piece of cake until you finish all your dinner." Ten minutes later your child still has not eaten any more of her food.

*Supportive words:*

# Bibliography

Hohmann, Mary, and David P. Weikart. 1995. *Educating Young Children: Active Learning Practices for Preschool and Child Care Programs.* Ypsilanti, MI: High/Scope Press.

Quick, Thomas. 1992. *Successful Team Building.* New York: AMACOM.

Scannell, Edward E., and John W. Newstrom. 1994. *Still More Games Trainers Play: Experiential Learning Exercises.* New York: McGraw-Hill, Inc.

*Supporting Children in Resolving Conflicts* (video). 1998. Available from High/Scope Press, 600 N. River, Ypsilanti, MI 48198.

Terdan, Susan M. 1996. "Celebrating With Preschoolers." In *Supporting Young Learners 2: Ideas for Child Care Providers and Teachers,* Nancy A. Brickman, ed., 247–254. Ypsilanti, MI: High/Scope Press.

# Index

# Workshop-Related High/Scope® Resources

## High/Scope's Preschool Manual and Study Guide

### Educating Young Children: Active Learning Practices for Preschool and Child Care Programs

This manual presents essential strategies adults can use to make active learning a reality in their programs. Covers key components of the adult's role, family involvement, daily team planning, creating interest areas, choosing appropriate materials, supporting the plan-do-review process, and arranging small- and large-group times.

**A6R-P1111 $39.95**

M. Hohmann & D. P. Weikart. Soft cover, 560 pages, 1995. 0-929816-91-9.

### A Study Guide to Educating Young Children: Exercises for Adult Learners

This workbook contains active-learning exercises exploring the content of the preschool manual in depth. Includes hands-on exploration of materials, child studies, analysis of photos and scenarios in EYC, recollection and reflection about curriculum topics, trying out support strategies, and making implementation plans. Chapter topics parallel EYC's.

**A6R-P1117 $15.95**

M. Hohmann. Soft cover, 275 pages, 1997. 1-57379-065-6.

## Children's Books

### Grandpa's Choice Series of Children's Books

Series editor, David P. Weikart. Translated from Dutch into English, these delightful storybooks explore children's fears, interests, friendships, and relationships. Order individual books or the whole series. **Each book $10.95. A6R-K1000SET $99.00.**

### High/Scope® Preschool Classroom Library Set of 55

The books in this set have been selected by High/Scope® educational consultants for their high-quality content, illustrations, and suitability for use in High/Scope® preschool settings. Buy a classroom set or any single title.

**A6R-PHB-55SET $680.56**

### High/Scope® Preschool Classroom Library Starter Set of 25

This set is a sub-set of our Preschool Classroom Library. It includes a variety of books that would serve as an ideal starter set for any preschool library.

**A6R-PHB-25SET $310.12**

### High/Scope's Favorite New Preschool Titles

Our Favorite New Preschool Titles include new books on the market that you may not be familiar with yet. As with our library sets, they were specially selected by High/Scope® educational consultants.

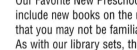

All children's books: 15% off list price. Please see our Web site or color catalog for the list of titles and the price list for our preschool children's book selections.

---

**To order these or any other High/Scope® products, contact High/Scope® Press: phone (800)40-PRESS fax (800)442-4FAX**

**To see a full listing of High/Scope® preschool products, visit our Web site: www.highscope.org**

# Workshop-Related High/Scope® Resources

## Videotapes

### Adult-Child Interactions: Forming Partnerships With Children

Shows teachers at High/Scope's Demonstration Preschool interacting as partners with children throughout the daily routine. Part 1 introduces interaction strategies, demonstrates their use in two work-time scenes, and includes a teacher commentary on each scene. Part 2 contains additional classroom scenes without commentary, to encourage viewer analysis and discussion.

**A6R-P1104 $50.95**

Video guide included. Color video, 60 minutes, 1996. 1-57379-022-2.

### Supporting Children in Resolving Conflicts

Teaches six problem-solving steps you can use to help children in conflict situations. The process is demonstrated with real scenes of successful conflict resolution from a New York City Head Start Center and from the High/Scope® Demonstration Preschool.

**A6R-P1130 $49.95**

Video guide included.
Color video, 24 minutes, 1998.
1-57379-042-7.

### The High/Scope® Curriculum: The Daily Routine

Shot entirely at High/Scope's Demonstration Preschool to highlight the rationale for each segment of the daily routine.

**A6R-P1082 $30.95**

Color video, 17 minutes, 1990.
0-929816-18-8.

### Supporting Children's Active Learning: Teaching Strategies for Diverse Settings

Highlights the many teaching styles you can adopt to facilitate children's active learning.

**A6R-P1077 $30.95**

Color video, 13 minutes, 1989.
0-929816-02-1.

## Other Materials

### High/Scope® Preschool Key Experience Chart

Easy-to-read, convenient wall chart listing all 58 High/Scope® preschool key experiences.

**A6R-P1110 $5.95** 22" x 34". 0-929816-97-8.

### 10 Preschool Key Experience Posters

Colorful posters to pin on your wall for daily inspiration. Each poster lists a major key experience category and contains a beautiful color photo for a quick reminder of active learning.

**A6R-P1125SETA $29.95**

Set of 10 posters,
each full-color poster 11" x 17".
1-57379-040-0.

### Wheel of Learning/Key Experience Card

Handy laminated reference tool containing complete listing of preschool key experiences on one side and wheel of learning on the other. Useful for child observations or for sharing with parents and other educators.

**A6R-P1113 $2.95** 8¹/₂" x 11". 0-929816-98-6.

### Steps in Resolving Conflicts Wall Chart

Handy reference tool to hang in the classroom to help you remember the six steps to resolving conflicts successfully as you work with children.

**A6R-P1134 $5.95**

2-color glossy, 22" x 34". 1-57379-075-3.

---

**To order these or any other High/Scope® products, contact High/Scope® Press: phone (800)40-PRESS fax (800)442-4FAX**
**To see a full listing of High/Scope® preschool products, visit our Web site: www.highscope.org**